Multilevel Activity Book

SERIES DIRECTOR
Jayme Adelson-Goldstein

4 **Chris Armen Mahdesian**

OXFORD
UNIVERSITY PRESS

OXFORD
UNIVERSITY PRESS

198 Madison Avenue
New York, NY 10016 USA

Great Clarendon Street, Oxford OX2 6DP UK

Oxford University Press is a department of the University of Oxford.
It furthers the University's objective of excellence in research, scholarship,
and education by publishing worldwide in

Oxford New York

Auckland Cape Town Dar es Salaam Hong Kong Karachi
Kuala Lumpur Madrid Melbourne Mexico City Nairobi
New Delhi Shanghai Taipei Toronto

With offices in

Argentina Austria Brazil Chile Czech Republic France Greece
Guatemala Hungary Italy Japan Poland Portugal Singapore
South Korea Switzerland Thailand Turkey Ukraine Vietnam

OXFORD and OXFORD ENGLISH are registered trademarks of
Oxford University Press

Executive Publisher: Janet Aitchison
Editorial Manager: Stephanie Karras
Senior Editor: Sharon Sargent
Art Director: Maj-Britt Hagsted
Senior Designer: Claudia Carlson
Art Editor: Robin Fadool
Production Manager: Shanta Persaud
Production Controller: Zai Jawat Ali

Printed in Hong Kong

10 9 8 7 6 5 4 3 2

ISBN: 978 0 19 439827 5

Acknowledgements

Illustrations by: John Batten, p.18, p.19, p.58, p.59, p.88, p.89, p,98, p.99,
p.110; Bill Dickson, p.20, p.38, p.39, p.68, p.69, p.80, p.100, p.130; Shawn
Banner, p.28, p.29, p.40, p.90, p.108, p.109; Kevin Brown, p.30, p.50, p.70,
p.120; Annie Bissett, p.36, p.86, p.126; Arlene Boehm, p.46, p.96; Laurie
Conley, p.48, p.49, p.60, p.78, p.79, p.128, p.129; Karen Minot, p.118,
p.119.

Photo by: Dennis Kitchen, p.1.

Many thanks to the Step Forward MLAB 4 team—
Janet, Stephanie, Sharon, Genevieve and Jayme.
Special gratitude to Amy, editor extraordinaire, for
making me a better writer.

This book is dedicated in memory of my grandmother
Nectar Mahdesian, a self-taught student of English who
endured many other hardships, and to my students for
many years of teaching and learning about so much in
addition to language.

Chris

Kudos to the amazing *Multilevel Activity Book 4*
team members who performed their assigned roles
with panache: Chris Mahdesian—inspired writer;
Amy Cooper—gifted facilitator; Maj-Britt Hagsted,
Claudia Carlson and Niki Barolini—artful designers;
Robin Fadool—resourceful picture finder; and
Sharon Sargent, Stephanie Karras and Janet Aitchison—
expert timekeepers and question askers.

To Sharon, the 8th wonder!

Jayme

Acknowledgments

The Publisher and Series Director would like to acknowledge the following individuals for their invaluable input during the development of this series:

Vittoria Abbatte-Maghsoudi Mount Diablo Unified School District, Loma Vista Adult Center, Concord, CA

Karen Abell Durham Technical Community College, Durham, NC

Millicent Alexander Los Angeles Unified School District, Huntington Park-Bell Community Adult School, Los Angeles, CA

Diana Allen Oakton Community College, Skokie, IL

Bethany Bandera Arlington Education and Employment Program, Arlington, VA

Sandra Bergman New York City Department of Education, New York, NY

Chan Bostwick Los Angeles Technology Center, Los Angeles, CA

Diana Brady-Herndon Napa Valley Adult School, Napa, CA

Susan Broellos Baldwin Park Unified School District, Baldwin Park, CA

Carmen Carbajal Mitchell Community College, Statesville, NC

Jose Carmona Daytona Beach Community College, Daytona Beach, FL

Ingrid Caswell Los Angeles Technology Center, Los Angeles, CA

Joyce Clapp Hayward Adult School, Hayward, CA

Beverly deNicola Capistrano Unified School District, San Juan Capistrano, CA

Edward Ende Miami Springs Adult Center, Miami Springs, FL

Gayle Fagan Harris County Department of Education, Houston, TX

Richard Firsten Lindsey Hopkins Technical Education Center, Miami, FL

Elizabeth Fitzgerald Hialeah Adult Center, Hialeah, FL

Mary Ann Florez Arlington Education and Employment Program, Arlington, VA

Leslie Foster Davidson Mitchell Community College, Statesville, NC

Beverly Gandall Santa Ana College School of Continuing Education, Santa Ana, CA

Rodriguez Garner Westchester Community College, Valhalla, NY

Sally Gearhart Santa Rosa Junior College, Santa Rosa, CA

Norma Guzman Baldwin Park Unified School District, Baldwin Park, CA

Lori Howard UC Berkeley, Education Extension, Berkeley, CA

Phillip L. Johnson Santa Ana College Centennial Education Center, Santa Ana, CA

Kelley Keith Mount Diablo Unified School District, Loma Vista Adult Center, Concord, CA

Blanche Kellawon Bronx Community College, Bronx, NY

Keiko Kimura Triton College, River Grove, IL

Jody Kirkwood ABC Adult School, Cerritos, CA

Matthew Kogan Evans Community Adult School, Los Angeles, CA

Laurel Leonard Napa Valley Adult School, Napa, CA

Barbara Linek Illinois Migrant Education Council, Plainfield, IL

Alice Macondray Neighborhood Centers Adult School, Oakland, CA

Ronna Magy Los Angeles Unified School District Central Office, Los Angeles, CA

Jose Marlasca South Area Adult Education, Melbourne, FL

Laura Martin Adult Learning Resource Center, Des Plaines, IL

Judith Martin-Hall Indian River Community College, Fort Pierce, FL

Michael Mason Mount Diablo Unified School District, Loma Vista Adult Center, Concord, CA

Katherine McCaffery Brewster Technical Center, Tampa, FL

Cathleen McCargo Arlington Education and Employment Program, Arlington, VA

Todd McDonald Hillsborough County Public Schools, Tampa, FL

Rita McSorley Northeast Independent School District, San Antonio, TX

Gloria Melendrez Evans Community Adult School, Los Angeles, CA

Vicki Moore El Monte-Rosemead Adult School, El Monte, CA

Meg Morris Mountain View Los Altos Adult Education District, Los Altos, CA

Nieves Novoa LaGuardia Community College, Long Island City, NY

Jo Pamment Haslett Public Schools, East Lansing, MI

Liliana Quijada-Black Irvington Learning Center, Houston, TX

Ellen Quish LaGuardia Community College, Long Island City, NY

Mary Ray Fairfax County Public Schools, Springfield, VA

Tatiana Roganova Hayward Adult School, Hayward, CA

Nancy Rogenscky-Roda Hialeah-Miami Lakes Adult Education and Community Center, Hialeah, FL

Lorraine Romero Houston Community College, Houston, TX

Edilyn Samways The English Center, Miami, FL

Kathy Santopietro Weddel Northern Colorado Literacy Program, Littleton, CO

Dr. G. Santos The English Center, Miami, FL

Fran Schnall City College of New York Literacy Program, New York, NY

Mary Segovia El Monte-Rosemead Adult School, El Monte, CA

Edith Smith City College of San Francisco, San Francisco, CA

Alisa Takeuchi Chapman Education Center Garden Grove, CA

Leslie Weaver Fairfax County Public Schools, Falls Church, VA

David Wexler Napa Valley Adult School, Napa, CA

Bartley P. Wilson Northeast Independent School District, San Antonio, TX

Emily Wonson Hunter College, New York, NY

Contents

Introduction............................1

Teaching Notes............................3

The First Step

Mixers

Why Are You Studying English? 13

What Are Your Favorite Things? 14

What Experiences Have You Had?............................ 15

What Are Your Hopes and Dreams? 16

Unit 1 It Takes All Kinds!

Lesson 1: Picture Differences

What Types of People Are They?

Picture A............................ 18

Picture B............................ 19

Lesson 2: Round Table Writing............................ 20

Different Kinds of Learners

Lesson 3

Peer Dictation: I Don't Even Own a Bicycle!.... 21

Survey: Are You Athletic?............................ 22

Lesson 4: Role-Play 23

Do You Agree or Disagree?

Lesson 5: Jigsaw Reading

Everybody Needs to Relax

Pair A............................ 24

Pair B............................ 25

Review and Expand

Team Project: What's Your Opinion? 26

Unit 2 Keeping Current

Lesson 1: Picture Differences

Did You See Today's Paper?

Picture A............................ 28

Picture B............................ 29

Lesson 2: Round Table Writing............................ 30

Who, What, When, Where, and Why?

Lesson 3

Peer Dictation: In the News............................ 31

Survey: What Can You Remember?............................ 32

Lesson 4: Role-Play 33

I Can Understand That

Lesson 5: Jigsaw Reading

Rescued by Their Pets!

Pair A............................ 34

Pair B............................ 35

Review and Expand

Team Project: Read All About It............................ 36

Unit 3 Going Places

Lesson 1: Picture Differences

Car Trouble!

Picture A............................ 38

Picture B............................ 39

Lesson 2: Round Table Writing............................ 40

Would You Like to Leave a Message?

Lesson 3

Peer Dictation: What Did They Say? 41

Survey: What Did You Say? 42

Lesson 4: Role-Play 43

Why Don't You Drive There?

Lesson 5: Jigsaw Reading

Telephones of Tomorrow

Pair A............................ 44

Pair B............................ 45

Review and Expand

Team Project: The Latest Thing
   for Travelers............................ 46

Unit 4 Get the Job

Lesson 1: Picture Differences

Steps to a Career

Picture A............................ 48

Picture B............................ 49

Lesson 2: Round Table Writing............................ 50

Job Skills to Go!

Lesson 3

Peer Dictation: What Had They Done? 51

Survey: I Had Never Learned That Before............................ 52

Lesson 4: Role-Play 53

Have You Had Any Training?

Lesson 5: Jigsaw Reading
Make or Break Your Next Interview!
Pair A.. 54
Pair B.. 55

Review and Expand
Team Project: The Right Person for the
    Right Job 56

Unit 5 Safe and Sound

Lesson 1: Picture Differences
Use Caution!
Picture A... 58
Picture B... 59

Lesson 2: Round Table Writing...................... 60
It's Good to Be Prepared.....................................

Lesson 3
Peer Dictation: Be Careful, Be Prepared............ 61
Survey: Things You've Got to Do........................ 62

Lesson 4: Role-Play 63
I'd Like to Report a Safety Hazard

Lesson 5: Jigsaw Reading
What Do You Know About Home Safety?
Pair A.. 64
Pair B.. 65

Review and Expand
Team Project: Safety Survey 66

Unit 6 Getting Ahead

Lesson 1: Picture Differences
Special Skills Make Special People
Picture A... 68
Picture B... 69

Lesson 2: Round Table Writing...................... 70
Employee of the Month

Lesson 3
Peer Dictation: The Best Employees 71
Survey: Interpersonal Skills 72

Lesson 4: Role-Play 73
Who Do I Talk to?

Lesson 5: Jigsaw Reading
Dealing with Difficult Co-workers
Pair A.. 74
Pair B.. 75

Review and Expand
Team Project: Know What to Do and Says........ 76

Unit 7 Buy Now, Pay Later

Lesson 1: Picture Differences
All About Finances
Picture A... 78
Picture B... 79

Lesson 2: Round Table Writing...................... 80
Can You Put a Price on Happiness?

Lesson 3
Peer Dictation: Time and Money 81
Survey: If You Won $1,000,000 82

Lesson 4: Role-Play 83
Let's Make It $150 a Month

Lesson 5: Jigsaw Reading
Super Savers
Pair A.. 84
Pair B.. 85

Review and Expand
Team Project: A Budget for Our Party 86

Unit 8 Satisfaction Guaranteed

Lesson 1: Picture Differences
Where Will She Find a Gift?
Picture A... 88
Picture B... 89

Lesson 2: Round Table Writing...................... 90
What a Disappointment!

Lesson 3
Peer Dictation: Not What They Expected......... 91
Survey: How Do You Feel About
    Shopping?... 92

Lesson 4: Role-Play 93
I'd Like to Place an Order

Lesson 5: Jigsaw Reading
Ask Mike Mechanic
Pair A.. 94
Pair B.. 95

Review and Expand
Team Project: Consumer's Choice..................... 96

Unit 9 Take Care!

Lesson 1: Picture Differences
Take Good Care of Yourself
Picture A... 98
Picture B... 99

Lesson 2: Round Table Writing........................ 100
Getting Started Was the Hardest Part

Lesson 3
Peer Dictation: A Lot of Advice 101
Survey: What You Should Do 102

Lesson 4: Role-Play 103
Is There Anything Else You'd Recommend?

Lesson 5: Jigsaw Reading
What's a Centenarian?
Pair A.. 104
Pair B.. 105

Review and Expand
Team Project: An Ounce of Prevention............ 106

Unit 10 Get Involved!

Lesson 1: Picture Differences
Make It Happen!
Picture A... 108
Picture B... 109

Lesson 2: Round Table Writing 110
They're Very Concerned

Lesson 3
Peer Dictation: Do You Have Any Idea? 111
Survey: Do You Where the Courthouse Is? 112

Lesson 4: Role-Play 113
I Understand What You're Saying

Lesson 5: Jigsaw Reading
Volunteers Make a Difference
Pair A.. 114
Pair B.. 115

Review and Expand
Team Project: Make a Difference 116

Unit 11 Find It on the Net

Lesson 1: Picture Differences
It's All on the Internet
Picture A... 118
Picture B... 119

Lesson 2: Round Table Writing 120
Some Things Will Never Change

Lesson 3
Peer Dictation: It Isn't Hard to Learn, Is It?.... 121
Survey: Using the Internet............................... 122

Lesson 4: Role-Play 123
Can I Offer a Suggestion?

Lesson 5: Jigsaw Reading
Tenant-Landlord Problems
Pair A.. 124
Pair B.. 125

Review and Expand
Team Project: Welcome to Our Website! 126

Unit 12 How Did I Do?

Lesson 1: Picture Differences
Congratulations!
Picture A... 128
Picture B... 129

Lesson 2: Round Table Writing 130
Past Achievements, Future Goals

Lesson 3
Peer Dictation: Oscar Isn't Afraid
     of Working Hard 131
Survey: Do You Believe in Setting Goals? 132

Lesson 4: Role-Play 133
You're Doing a Great Job!

Lesson 5: Jigsaw Reading
Old Products, New Ideas
Pair A.. 134
Pair B.. 135

Review and Expand
Team Project: What's My Profession?.............. 136

Introduction to the *Step Forward Multilevel Activity Book 4*

Welcome to the *Step Forward Multilevel Activity Book 4*. In these pages you'll find a wealth of highly interactive activities that require little preparation. All of the activities can be used in numerous ways with a variety of learners. The 76 activities in this book are effective in high-intermediate classes as well as in multilevel classes with learners ranging from high-beginning to low-advanced levels.

This book is divided into 12 units that directly correspond to *Step Forward Student Book 4*. Each activity supports and expands upon the student book's lesson objectives, for a complete approach to English language learning.

1 What is the Multilevel Activity Book?

The *Multilevel Activity Book 4* (like the entire *Step Forward* series) is based on research that says adults taught in a learner-centered classroom retain more material for longer periods of time (McCombs and Whistler 1997, Benson and Voller 1997). Through its guided and communicative practice opportunities, the *Multilevel Activity Book 4* provides hours of meaningful and fun classroom activities.

2 How do I use these reproducible activities?

The Teaching Notes on pages 3–11 give detailed directions on how to conduct each activity and also provide multilevel suggestions. They guide you through

1. setting up the activity,
2. modeling/demonstrating the activity,
3. checking your learners' comprehension of each activity's goal and directions.

Once learners understand how to proceed, they are able to work together to complete the activities. Putting learning into the learners' hands is an important step towards ensuring that they will achieve the lesson objective. Moving away from the front-and-center role frees you to circulate, monitor, facilitate, and gain insight into how well the lesson information was captured. You discover what learners can and can't do well, and adjust your future lesson plans accordingly.

3 What makes these activities multilevel?

One of the key techniques in multilevel instruction is to use materials that can work across levels. There are eight activity types in this book. Each one allows you to target practice to the learner's abilities, but still have the entire class working on the same basic activity. (See the photo below for an example.) Having only eight activity types means that students quickly understand how to do the activities, requiring less teacher intervention and more learner-directed

The Jigsaw Readings in *Multilevel Activity Book 4* allow learners to work at their own level and pace. Higher-level pairs use more complex language to talk about the readings while lower-level pairs use simpler language to perform the same task.

practice. Each activity includes a Keep Going suggestion for a follow-up activity, such as discussing answers, sharing opinions about a related topic or reporting on a task. The eight activity types are described below.

ACTIVITY	GROUPING STRATEGY	DESCRIPTION	CORRELATION TO Step Forward Student Book 4
Mixer	Whole Class	Learners get acquainted as they ask and answer questions.	**Pre-unit: The First Step**
Picture Differences	Pairs	Learners reinforce their understanding of target words and phrases by identifying differences between two pictures.	**Lesson 1: Vocabulary**
Round Table Writing	Small groups	Learners take turns writing sentences that complete a story about a picture.	**Lesson 2: Real-life writing**
Peer Dictation	Pairs	Partners take turns dictating sentences that reinforce grammar structures while developing their clarification strategies.	**Lesson 3: Grammar**
Survey	Whole Class; Pairs	Learners gather classmates' information and write sentences about the results.	**Lesson 3: Grammar**
Role-Play	Small Groups	Learners develop fluency by practicing and expanding upon conversation gambits.	**Lesson 4: Everyday conversation**
Jigsaw Reading	Pairs	Partners read a high-interest text and answer questions. They then work with another pair to learn about that pair's reading and answer questions about their own.	**Lesson 5: Real-life reading**
Team Project	Small Groups	Learners work together to complete a project.	**Review and expand**

By having pairs or small groups practice the language required to meet a lesson objective, teachers facilitate learners' use and internalization of the target language. This also provides important opportunities for learners to engage in real-life interaction strategies such as negotiating meaning, checking information, disagreeing, and reaching consensus.

While a pair of running shoes is not required equipment, most multilevel instructors find themselves on the move in the classroom.

These highly structured activities support the energetic, communicative, and lively approach to learning that is the hallmark of effective multilevel instruction. The Step Forward Team hopes that you and your learners enjoy these activities.

Please write to us with your comments and questions: **Stepforwardteam.us@oup.com.**

Jayme Adelson-Goldstein, Series Director

Multilevel Activity Teaching Notes

Pre-unit: The First Step: Mixer Teaching Notes.................. 4

Lesson 1: Picture Differences Teaching Notes 5

Lesson 2: Round Table Writing Teaching Notes 6

Lesson 3:
Peer Dictation Teaching Notes 7
Survey Teaching Notes 8

Lesson 4: Role-Play Teaching Notes 9

Lesson 5: Jigsaw Reading Teaching Notes............................10

Review and Expand
Team Project Teaching Notes 11

Teaching Notes for the Mixer

Focus: Students get to know each other by asking and answering questions.
Grouping Strategy: Whole class
Activity Time: 25–30 minutes
Student Book Connection: Pre-unit The First Step

Ready,

1. Select a Mixer activity.

2. Duplicate one activity page for each student.

3. Write the question(s) from Step 1 of the Mixer on the board.

Set...

1. Share the goal of the activity: *You're going to talk to your classmates to learn more about each other.*

2. Have a higher-level volunteer ask the question(s) on the board.

3. Elicit responses to the question(s) on the board from the class.

4. Distribute an activity page to each student and review the directions.

5. As indicated in the directions, ask students to add one or more questions of their own.

6. Ask two volunteers to come to the front and model the activity, using the first Mixer question.

7. Check students' comprehension by asking *yes/no* questions. *Do you answer the questions yourself?* [no]

Go!

1. Set a time limit (five minutes).

2. Have students circulate to complete the activity page. Tell them to sit down when their activity page is complete and have them write sentences about their classmates, using the information from the survey.

3. Give students a two-minute warning.

4. Call "time."

Keep Going!

Have students complete the Keep Going activity on the Mixer page.

Multilevel Suggestions

Before the Activity:

Pre-Level: Help students read the questions and write their own answers in their notebooks. Pair each pre-level student with a higher-level student. Have the partners work together to write the additional question(s).

On-Level: Have students read the questions and write their answers in their notebooks. Have students write the additional question(s) independently.

Higher-Level: Have students write the additional question(s) independently, and then help the pre-level students write their question(s).

Teaching Notes for the Picture Differences

Focus: Students work together to find ten differences between two pictures.
Grouping Strategy: Pairs
Activity Time: 20–25 minutes
Student Book Connection: Lesson 1

Ready,

1. Select the Picture Differences activity that corresponds to the unit you are teaching in *Step Forward Student Book 4*.

2. Duplicate one set of activity pages for each pair of students.

3. Check the picture differences yourself to determine what, if any, new vocabulary students will need in order to communicate the differences. Introduce new vocabulary as needed.

4. Draw a simple picture on the left side of the board (such as a stick figure). Draw the picture again on the right side of the board, this time with one difference (such as the stick figure wearing a hat). Ask students to identify the difference between the two pictures and to describe the pictures in sentence form. Write the students' sentences under the pictures. Picture A: *The man isn't wearing a hat.* Picture B: *The man is wearing a hat.*

Set...

1. Share the goal of the activity: *You're going to work together to find the differences between your pictures. This will help you practice vocabulary.*

2. Have two volunteers demonstrate the activity.
- Identify one student as Partner A and the other as Partner B.
- Give Picture A to Partner A and the other to Partner B. Tell them not to look at each other's papers.
- Have the partners ask and answer questions about each other's pictures and find a difference between them. *In my picture, Ana is jogging. Is she jogging in your picture? No, in my picture, Ana is talking.*
- Have the partners work together to write two sentences that describe the picture difference that they found.

3. Pair students, assign *A/B* roles, and distribute one set of activity pages to each pair.

4. Review the directions.

5. Check comprehension by asking pre-level students *yes/no* questions: *Do you show your partner your picture?* [no] Ask on-level and higher-level students information questions: *How many differences should you find?* [10]

Go!

1. Set a time limit (ten minutes).

2. A/B pairs work together, identifying the picture differences and writing sentences to describe these differences. Students continue until they've identified ten differences between the pictures and written two sentences for each difference (a total of twenty sentences).

3. Monitor progress and assist students as needed.

4. Call "time." Have volunteers write their sentences on the board and then have the class correct spelling as needed.

Keep Going!

Have students talk about a picture-related topic, using the discussion prompt on the activity page.

Multilevel Suggestions

For Mixed-Level Pairs:
Tell pre-level students they can write incomplete sentences. Have on-level and higher-level students help their pre-level group members write complete grammatical sentences.

For Same-Level Pairs:
Pre-Level: Before pre-level students begin the activity, review the key vocabulary for the items in the pictures. Allow pre-level students to look at each other's papers and to express differences with sentence fragments rather than full sentences.

On-Level: Have students complete the activity as outlined above.

Higher-Level: Have higher-level students write as many sentences as they can about things that are the same in the pictures.

Teaching Notes for the Round Table Writing

Focus: Students study a picture and then take turns writing sentences to complete a story about it.
Grouping Strategy: Groups of 4 students
Activity Time: 25–30 minutes
Student Book Connection: Lesson 2

Ready,

1. Select the Round Table Writing activity that corresponds to the unit you are teaching in *Step Forward Student Book 4*.

2. Duplicate one activity page for every four students.

3. On the board, draw a simple picture and write a sample sentence that could be the first line in a story about the picture.

4. Provide a review of the vocabulary and concepts represented in the Round Table Writing picture.

Set...

1. Share the goal of the activity: *You're going to brainstorm sentences about a picture. Then you're going to take turns writing sentences to complete a story about the picture.*

2. Form groups of four students.

3. Model the activity, using the picture and the sample sentence on the board. Ask a few volunteers to brainstorm more sentences about the picture. Write the volunteers' sentences on the board.

4. Work with the class to number the sentences in order. Cross out any repetitive sentences.

5. Ask a volunteer to continue the story by writing the first sentence in the numbered sequence (see Step 4, above) after the sample sentence.

6. Distribute one activity page to each group and review the directions.

7. Check comprehension by asking *yes/no* questions. *Do you write all of the sentences yourself?* [no] *Should all of the sentences tell a story about the picture?* [yes]

8. Have students, in their groups, read the sample sentence silently as you read it aloud.

Go!

1. Set a time limit (five minutes) for students to brainstorm sentences about the picture.

2. Call "time," and set a time limit (fifteen minutes) for students to number their sentences in order, cross out any repetitive sentence, and take turns writing sentences to continue the story.

3. Monitor the groups' progress. Assist students as needed.

4. Once a group is finished writing, have them read through their story, identify the words they're unsure of, and assign each group member one or more words to check in the dictionary.

5. Call "time."

Keep Going!

Have each group exchange stories with another group. Students read the other group's story and discuss it, based on the question in the prompt. Repeat the exchange and discussion process at least twice.

Multilevel Suggestions

For Mixed-Level Groups:
Tell pre-level students they can write incomplete sentences. Instruct on-level and higher-level students to help their pre-level group members write complete grammatical sentences.

For Same-Level Groups:

Pre-Level: Review and write on the board the vocabulary that students will need in order to complete the activity. You may also wish to ask students questions about the picture. Such questions will help students construct their own sentences.

On-Level: Have students complete the activity as outlined above.

Higher-Level: Before assigning the activity to these students, provide several prompts that will encourage students to write sentences based on their ideas and opinions. For example, *Have you ever been in this situation? What is your opinion of what the man is doing? If you were in this situation, what would you do?*

Teaching Notes for the Peer Dictation

Focus: Students dictate sentences to each other to complete the activity page.
Grouping Strategy: Pairs
Activity Time: 15-25 minutes
Student Book Connection: Lesson 3

Ready,

1. Select the Peer Dictation activity that corresponds to the unit you are teaching in *Step Forward Student Book 4*.

2. Duplicate one activity page for each student.

3. On the left side of the board, write a sentence that relates to the topic. Label this side of the board *Partner A*. Label the right side of the board *Partner B*.

4. Familiarize students with the dictation process by asking volunteers to read the sentence on the left side of the board to you. Before you write the sentence on the board, repeat it back, incorrectly. Encourage students to correct you by reading the sentence to you again. Next, repeat the sentence correctly, and write it on the right side of the board.

Set...

1. Share the goal of the activity: *You're going to practice reading, listening to, and writing sentences.*

2. Have one volunteer pair model the activity for the class. Ask the pair to come to the front and sit across from each other. Give each partner one of the activity pages. Tell the partners what to do as the class watches and listens.
- *Fold your papers.*
- *Partner A, look at the top. Partner B, look at the bottom.*
- *Partner A, read the first sentence on the page to your partner.*
- *Partner B, repeat what you hear.*
- *Partner A, confirm that Partner B heard the sentence correctly.*
- *Partner B, write the sentence.*

3. When A finishes, have B dictate the first sentence on the bottom half of the sheet to A.

4. Distribute one activity page per person and review the directions.

5. Pair students, assign *A/B* roles, and have them fold their activity pages.

6. Check comprehension by asking *or* questions. *Do you fold or cut the paper?* [fold] *Does Partner A read the A sentences or the B sentences?* [the A sentences]

Go!

1. Set a time limit (five minutes) for A to dictate to B.

2. Call "time" and set a time limit (five minutes) for B to dictate to A.

3. Call "time" and have pairs unfold their papers and check their work.

Keep Going!

Have students each write five sentences on the topic suggested in the prompt. Point out the example sentence, and encourage students to use the target grammar. Have students talk about their sentences with a partner. Have each pair dictate one of their sentences to the class.

Multilevel Suggestions

For Mixed-Level Pairs:
Pair on-level or higher-level students with pre-level students. Allow pre-level students to either write or to dictate, depending on what they would rather do.

For Same-Level Pairs:
Pre-Level: Provide a simplified version of the peer dictation by covering a few key words or phrases in each sentence on the activity page and then duplicating it for the students. Conduct the activity as outlined above.

On-Level: Have students complete the activity as outlined above.

Higher-Level: Review the information question words: *who, what, where, when.* Direct students to purposely obscure one of the words in each sentence as they dictate. This will force their partner to clarify before they write. Partner A: *My friends* [mumble: *Ria and Abu*] *are very athletic people.* Partner B: *Who are very athletic people?*

Teaching Notes for the Survey

Focus: Students conduct a survey and then write sentences about the results.
Grouping Strategy: Whole class, Pairs
Activity Time: 30–40 minutes
Student Book Connection: Lesson 3

Ready,

1. Select the Survey activity that corresponds to the unit you are teaching in *Step Forward Student Book 4.*

2. Duplicate one activity page for each student.

3. Draw a simplified chart on the board based on the first row of the survey chart.

4. Ask the first survey question and answer it yourself. Put your answer under the "My answers" column of the chart.

5. Ask three students the same question, and fill in their responses on the chart.

Set...

1. Share the goal of the activity: *You're going to ask and answer questions about ____ with your classmates. Then you're going to work with a partner. You will compare your classmates' answers and write sentences about them.*

2. Distribute one activity page per person and review the directions. Check comprehension by asking information questions. *Who answers each question first?* [I do.] *How many other students do you interview for each question?* [three]

3. Have students silently read and respond to the survey questions, marking their responses in the column titled "My answers."

4. Set a time limit (ten minutes).

Go!

1. Direct students to interview three other students and to write the responses of those students in the chart.

2. Set a time limit (10 minutes).

3. Circulate and monitor students' progress.

4. Call "time."

5. Have students sit with a partner to compare their charts and write sentences about their comparison. Set a time limit (5 minutes).

6. Assist students as needed.

Keep Going!

Have students talk about the topic using the discussion prompt on the activity page.

Multilevel Suggestions

For Mixed-Level Groups:
To help pre-level students fully participate in the survey, duplicate the activity page in three colors. Distribute one color to pre-level students, one color to on-level students, and one to higher-level students. Tell students they can only survey students with a different color paper.

For Same-Level Groups:
Pre-Level: Students can answer questions with short answers or sentence fragments.

On-Level: Have students complete the activity as outlined above. Encourage students to use the target grammar in their responses.

Higher-Level: Encourage students to ask each other two or three follow-up questions.

Teaching Notes for the Role Play

Focus: Working in groups, students read, choose roles, write the ending, and act out a role-play.
Grouping Strategy: Groups of 3-4 students.
Activity Time: 45–60 minutes
Student Book Connection: Lesson 4

Ready,

1. Select the Role Play activity that corresponds to the unit you are teaching in *Step Forward Student Book 4*.

2. Duplicate one activity page for each student.

3. Check the "Props" list to determine what items you need to bring to class. You will need one set of props for every two-to-three students.

4. Check the script to determine what, if any, new vocabulary students will need in order to do the role-play.

Set...

1. Share the goal of the activity: *You're going to work in groups and act out different parts in a role-play.*

2. Have students form groups according to the number of characters.

3. Distribute one activity page per person and one set of props per group. Review the directions: *First read the script. Next decide who will play each character. Then write an ending. You must add more lines for each character.*

4. Present new vocabulary or review vocabulary as needed.

5. Check comprehension by asking *yes/no* questions. *Do you say all the lines?* [no] *Do you act out your lines?* [yes]

6. Invite two volunteers to the front. Have each pick a line of dialog from the script and act it out for the class.

Go!

1. Set a time limit (fifteen minutes) for the group to read the script, choose their characters, and finish the role-play.

2. Set a time limit (five minutes) and have the students act out the role-play in their groups.

3. Monitor student's progress by walking around and helping with problems such as register or pronunciation (rhythm, stress, and intonation). Encourage pantomime and improvisation.

Keep Going!

Have each group perform their role-play for the class. Ask students, while watching the role-plays, to write the answers to the questions in the Keep Going section on the activity page.

Multilevel Suggestions

For Mixed-Level Groups:
Adapt the role-play to include a more limited speaking role for pre-level students who are not ready to participate fully. For example, add a character who only gives short answers to questions asked by another character. In larger classes, you may want to assign a higher-level student as a "director" for each group.

For Same-Level Groups:
Pre-Level: On the board, write a simplified conversation based on the role-play situation. Help students read and copy the conversation in their notebooks. Then have pairs practice the conversation until they can perform it without the script.

On-Level: Have students complete the activity as outlined above.

Higher-Level: Have students create their own version of the role-play using related vocabulary or a similar situation.

Teaching Notes for the Jigsaw Reading

Focus: Students read a text and exchange information with another pair who read a complimentary text.
Grouping Strategy: Pairs
Activity Time: 30–40 minutes
Student Book Connection: Lesson 5

Ready,

1. Select the Jigsaw Readings that correspond to the unit you are teaching in *Step Forward Student Book 4.*

2. Duplicate one set of activity pages for every four students. Using different color paper for the A and B articles makes it easier to group students.

3. Model the general concept of the Jigsaw Reading by doing the following: Ask four volunteers to turn their backs to the board. Label the left side of the board *Pair A*. Write a simple sentence on this side, such as *Mark lives in Chicago*. Label the right side of the board *Pair B*. On this side, write a question relating to Pair A's sentence, such as *Where does Mark live?* Lead two volunteers to each side of the board, telling them to read silently only what is on their side. Ask Pair B to ask their question. Prompt Pair A to answer with the information from their sentence. Ask B to write the answer below the question on the board. You may wish to repeat this process with a Pair B "reading" and a Pair A question. *Pair B: Alma works in a restaurant. Pair A: What does Alma do?*

Set...

1. Share the goal of the activity: *You're going to practice reading, and then asking and answering questions about what you read.*

2. Present new vocabulary or review vocabulary as needed.

3. Have half the students seated on one side of the room pair up as "A" partners. Have students on the other side of the room pair up as "B" partners. Distribute the A activity pages to each member of the A pairs, and the B activity pages to each member of the B pairs.

4. Review the directions for Steps 1, 2, and 3.

5. Check comprehension by asking *yes/no* questions. *Do you read both articles?* [no] *Do you ask questions about your partner's article?* [yes]

Go!

1. Set a time limit (five minutes) for the students to read their text. Observe students during silent reading, and assist any pairs who need help with vocabulary or comprehension.

2. Call time and have partners answer the questions in Step 3. Remind students that they will have to teach two other students about their article.

3. Call time and have A pairs stand up and find B pairs to work with. Instruct the two sets of pairs to sit together. Review the directions for Steps 4 and 5. Check comprehension. *Do you ask questions?* [yes] *Do you read your article to the other pair?* [no]

4. Set a time limit (five minutes) for Pair B to ask Pair A questions about the A article.

5. Call time and set another time limit (five minutes) for Pair A to ask Pair B questions about the B article. Remind students that everyone in the group should be able to answer both sets of questions.

Keep Going!

Have students use the discussion prompt on the activity page to talk about a topic related to the articles.

Multilevel Suggestions

For Mixed-Level Pairs:
Pair each pre-level student with an on- or higher-level student. Have the higher-level student help the pre-level student with vocabulary and comprehension during the reading.

For Same-Level Pairs:
Pre-Level: Work with the pre-level pairs while the other groups are reading, and help them with vocabulary and comprehension as needed. Simplify the questions students ask and answer by changing them from information questions to *yes/no* questions. For example, the information question *Where does Alma live?* could be simplified to the *yes/no* question *Does Alma live in New York City?*

On-Level: Have pairs complete the project as outlined above.

Higher-Level: Provide additional questions for these students to ask each other, and/or have them add their own questions. Have students teach each other about their articles without looking back at their papers.

Teaching Notes for the Team Project

Focus: Students work in a team to complete a project-based learning exercise.
Grouping Strategy: Teams of 3-5 students
Activity Time: 60 minutes
Student Book Connection: Review and Expand

Ready,

1. Select the Team Project activity that corresponds to the unit you're teaching in *Step Forward Student Book 4*.

2. Duplicate one copy of the activity page for each student.

3. Check the supplies and the resources needed for the project and gather enough for each team.

4. If possible, create a sample of the project students will be doing (e.g., a webpage or an advertisement).

5. Provide a review of the vocabulary and concepts students will need to complete the project.

Set...

1. Share the goal of the activity: *You're going to work in teams to create* [product]. If you have created a sample of the product, show it to the students and answer any questions about it.

2. Have students form teams of three, four, or five. Explain the roles for the activity (see the individual activity page). Allow students to choose their jobs.

3. Ask the Supplier to pick up activity pages for his/her team.

4. As the Leaders to read the directions to their team.

5. Check comprehension by asking *yes/no* questions. *Does one person do all the work?* [no] *Do you make a list of ideas?* [yes]

6. Set a time limit (five minutes) for teams to brainstorm ideas. The Recorder writes the team's ideas while the Leader watches the clock.

Go!

1. Have students begin to create their projects. Tell students they will have 25-30 minutes to complete the project.

2. Circulate to check each team's progress.

3. About twenty minutes into the time period, check with teams to see if they need more time. Extend the time limit by five or ten minutes as needed.

4. Call "time." Have the Reporter from each team tell the class about their project.

Keep Going!

Have students complete the Keep Going activity on the Team Project activity page.

Multilevel Suggestions

For Mixed-Level Groups:
Assign pre-level students to roles that require less reading, writing, and speaking such as Supplier, Artist, and Graphic Designer. Ask higher-level students to be Leaders and Recorders.

For Same-Level Groups:
Pre-Level: Simplify the project by reducing the amount of reading and writing required. For example, for a newspaper project, have students write only headlines and captions for pictures.

On-Level: Have teams complete the project as outlined above.

Higher-Level: Increase the challenge for students by requiring more writing on the project. For example, have students write a paragraph on how well their team worked together or what they learned from the project.

Pre-unit The First Step

Mixers

Why Are You Studying English? 13

What Are Your Favorite Things? 14

What Experiences Have You Had? 15

What Are Your Hopes and Dreams? 16

Why Are You Studying English?

1. Think about this question: Why are you studying English?
2. Read the questions in the chart. Write 2 more questions for each section.
3. Walk around the room. Find 1 classmate who answers *yes* and 1 classmate who answers *no* to each question.

   Are you studying English to prepare for a job interview?
   Yes, I am. / No, I'm not.

4. Write your classmates' names in the correct boxes.

	Are you studying English to _____?	Classmates' Names	
		Yes	No
Work	prepare for a job interview?		
	communicate better with customers?		
Home	improve your telephone skills?		
	understand information on packages of food, medicine, and other products for the home?		
Community	prepare for citizenship?		
	get more involved in your community?		
Self	read the newspaper?		
	make new friends?		

KEEP GOING!

Work with a partner. Compare your charts. In each section, what is the most important reason for studying English?

What Are Your Favorite Things?

1. Think about this question: What are some of your favorite things?

2. Read the questions in the chart. Add 2 more questions.

3. Walk around the room. Ask and answer the questions.

What is your favorite food?
Cheese.

4. Write your classmates' names and answers in the correct boxes.

What is your favorite...	_____'s answers	_____'s answers	_____'s answers	_____'s answers
food?				
sport?				
city?				
holiday?				
month of the year?				
recreational activity?				
type of music?				
TV program?				
type of animal?				
type of weather?				

KEEP GOING!

Work with a partner. Choose one question. Look at your charts to see how your classmates answered the question. Make a bar graph to show the results.

What Experiences Have You Had?

1. Think about this question: What are some interesting experiences you have had?

2. Read the questions. Add 2 more questions.

3. Walk around the room. Ask questions to learn about your classmates' experiences.

Have you ever lived on a farm?
Yes, I have. / No, I haven't.

4. Check *yes* or *no*. Write a different name on each line.

1. Have you ever lived on a farm?

☐ Yes _____
(name)

☐ No _____
(name)

2. Have you ever been on TV?

☐ Yes _____
(name)

☐ No _____
(name)

3. Have you ever had a dog?

☐ Yes _____
(name)

☐ No _____
(name)

4. Have you ever been to a surprise party?

☐ Yes _____
(name)

☐ No _____
(name)

5. Have you ever _____?

☐ Yes _____
(name)

☐ No _____
(name)

6. Have you ever _____?

☐ Yes _____
(name)

☐ No _____
(name)

KEEP GOING!
Work with a partner. Tell your partner more about one of your experiences.

What Are Your Hopes and Dreams?

1. Think about this question: What are some of your hopes and dreams?

2. Read the questions. Add 2 more questions.

3. Walk around the room. Ask questions to learn about your classmates' hopes and dreams.

What activity have you always wanted to try?
Mountain climbing.

4. Write your classmates' names and answers in the correct boxes.

Ask and answer these questions.	_____'s answers	_____'s answers	_____'s answers	_____'s answers
What activity have you always wanted to try?				
Where have you always wanted to live?				
What is your dream job?				
What city have you always wanted to visit?				
What language have you always wanted to learn?				
Where do you hope to take your next vacation?				

KEEP GOING!

Ask your teacher a question from the mixer.

Unit 1 It Takes All Kinds!

Lesson 1: Picture Differences
What Types of People Are They?
Picture A...18
Picture B...19

Lesson 2: Round Table Writing...20
Different Kinds of Learners

Lesson 3
Peer Dictation: I Don't Even Own a Bicycle! 21
Survey: Are You Athletic?..22

Lesson 4: Role-Play...23
Do You Agree or Disagree?

Lesson 5: Jigsaw Reading
Everybody Needs to Relax
Pair A 24
Pair B 25

Review and Expand
Team Project: What's Your Opinion? 26

Picture A: What Types of People Are They?

1. Find a partner with Picture B (page 19). Don't show this paper to your partner!

2. Work with your partner to find 10 differences between your pictures.

3. Write the picture differences in the chart below.

	Picture A	**Picture B**
1.	*Ana is social.*	*Ana is athletic.*
2.		
3.		
4.		
5.		
6.		
7.		
8.		
9.		
10.		

KEEP GOING!
Talk about different personality types. What types of people are your friends?

Picture B: What Types of People Are They?

1. Find a partner with Picture A (page 18). Don't show this paper to your partner!

2. Work with your partner to find 10 differences between your pictures.

3. Write the picture differences in the chart below.

	Picture A	Picture B
1.	*Ana is social.*	*Ana is athletic.*
2.		
3.	.	
4.		
5.		
6.		
7.		
8.		
9.		
10.		

KEEP GOING!
Talk about different personality types. What types of people are your friends?

Unit 1 Picture Differences   **19**

Different Kinds of Learners

1. Work with 3 classmates.
2. Look at the picture. Read the first sentence.
3. Brainstorm sentences about the picture.
4. Take turns writing sentences to continue the story.
5. Check your spelling in a dictionary.

Different people learn new information in different ways.

_____

_____

_____

_____

_____

_____

_____

KEEP GOING!

Exchange stories with another group. What do you find interesting, surprising, or funny about their story?

I Don't Even Own a Bicycle!

Partner A
• **Read a sentence to Partner B.** • **Listen to Partner B repeat the sentence.**   **Is it correct? If not, say it again.**
1. My friend Tony is the most artistic person in our school. 2. He paints and draws all the time. 3. Everybody loves his interesting photographs, too. 4. I think he'll be a famous artist someday.
• **Listen to Partner B say a sentence.** • **Repeat the sentence.** • **Write the sentence.**
5.
6.
7.
8.

- - - - - - - - - - - - - - - - FOLD HERE- - - - - - - - - - - - - - - - -

Partner B
• **Listen to Partner A say a sentence.** • **Repeat the sentence.** • **Write the sentence.**
1.
2.
3.
4.
• **Read a sentence to Partner A.** • **Listen to Partner A repeat the sentence.**   **Is it correct? If not, say it again.**
5. My friends Ria and Abu are very athletic people. 6. They ride their bikes twenty miles every weekend. 7. They've invited me to go with them next Saturday. 8. Unfortunately, I don't even own a bicycle!

KEEP GOING!

Write 5 sentences to describe people you know. Talk about the sentences with your partner.

My friend Rita knows a lot about U.S. history.

Are You Athletic?

1. Read the questions. Write your answers in the chart.
2. Ask your classmates the questions in the chart.
3. Write your classmates' names and answers in the chart.
4. Use complete sentences to answer your classmates' questions.

Ask and answer these questions.	My answers	_____'s answers	_____'s answers	_____'s answers
Are you athletic?				
Do you believe exercise is important?				
What form of exercise do you like most?				
Do you own any exercise equipment?				
What is one thing you don't like about exercise?				

5. Work with a partner. Compare your charts. Write 6 sentences.

   Pedro and Richard are athletic, but Lee isn't.

1. _____
2. _____
3. _____
4. _____
5. _____
6. _____

KEEP GOING!
How can exercise improve people's lives? Talk about your opinions with the class.

Do You Agree or Disagree?

1. Work with 2 classmates. Say all the lines in the script.
2. Choose your character.
3. Finish the conversation. Write more lines for each character.
4. Practice the lines.
5. Act out the role-play with your group.

Scene	**Characters**	**Props**
A school cafeteria	• Student 1 • Student 2 • Student 3	Coffee cups

The Script

Student 1: What are you two discussing?

Student 2: We're just having a conversation about learning English.

Student 3: Well, I think there should be an "English Only" rule in class.

Student 1: You mean students should only speak English and no other language?

Student 3: Yes, that's the idea. Do you agree or disagree?

Student 1: I agree. If you only speak English, you learn English faster.

Student 2: You have a point, but sometimes translating words is faster.

Student 3: It may be faster, but then you're not practicing English skills.

Student 1: That's true.

Student 2: So, do you think students should use dictionaries in class?

KEEP GOING!

Watch your classmates' role-plays. Write the answers to these questions: What are the students' opinions about using dictionaries in class? Which opinion do you agree with?

Pair A: Everybody Needs to Relax

1. Find a partner with page 24. You are Pair A.

2. Read the article.

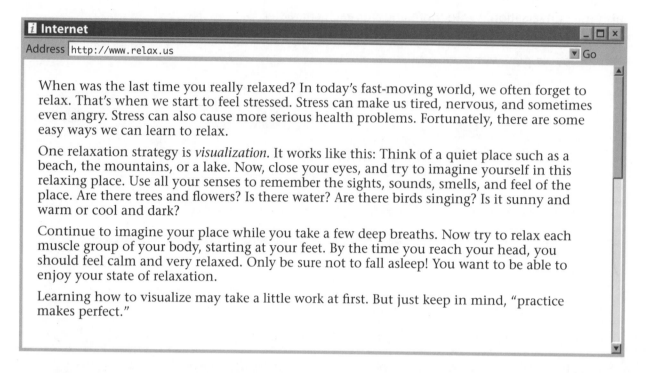

i Internet   `_ □ x`

Address `http://www.relax.us`   ▼ Go

When was the last time you really relaxed? In today's fast-moving world, we often forget to relax. That's when we start to feel stressed. Stress can make us tired, nervous, and sometimes even angry. Stress can also cause more serious health problems. Fortunately, there are some easy ways we can learn to relax.

One relaxation strategy is *visualization*. It works like this: Think of a quiet place such as a beach, the mountains, or a lake. Now, close your eyes, and try to imagine yourself in this relaxing place. Use all your senses to remember the sights, sounds, smells, and feel of the place. Are there trees and flowers? Is there water? Are there birds singing? Is it sunny and warm or cool and dark?

Continue to imagine your place while you take a few deep breaths. Now try to relax each muscle group of your body, starting at your feet. By the time you reach your head, you should feel calm and very relaxed. Only be sure not to fall asleep! You want to be able to enjoy your state of relaxation.

Learning how to visualize may take a little work at first. But just keep in mind, "practice makes perfect."

3. Answer the QUESTIONS FOR PAIR A together.

QUESTIONS FOR PAIR A

  a. When you practice visualization, what do you think about?

  _____

  b. What do you use all your senses to remember?

  _____

  c. What else do you do during visualization?

  _____

4. Find a Pair B with page 25. Answer their questions about your article.

5. Ask them the QUESTIONS TO ASK PAIR B. Write their answers.

QUESTIONS TO ASK PAIR B

  a. How do most people breathe when they are stressed?

  _____

  b. What kind of breathing helps the body relax?

  _____

  c. Describe the steps of deep breathing.

  _____

KEEP GOING!

Talk about other relaxation strategies. What strategies work best for you?

Pair B: Everybody Needs to Relax

1. Find a partner with page 25. You are Pair B.

2. Read the article.

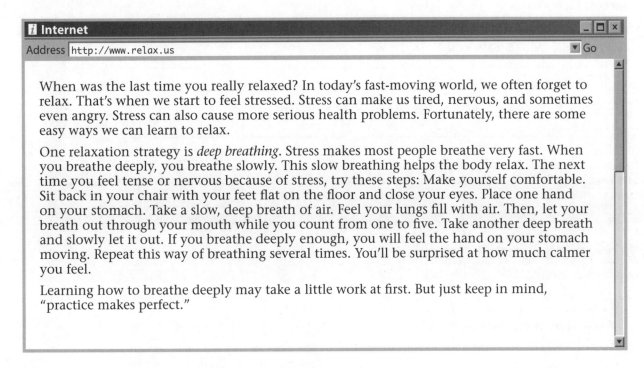

i Internet

Address http://www.relax.us   ▼ Go

When was the last time you really relaxed? In today's fast-moving world, we often forget to relax. That's when we start to feel stressed. Stress can make us tired, nervous, and sometimes even angry. Stress can also cause more serious health problems. Fortunately, there are some easy ways we can learn to relax.

One relaxation strategy is *deep breathing*. Stress makes most people breathe very fast. When you breathe deeply, you breathe slowly. This slow breathing helps the body relax. The next time you feel tense or nervous because of stress, try these steps: Make yourself comfortable. Sit back in your chair with your feet flat on the floor and close your eyes. Place one hand on your stomach. Take a slow, deep breath of air. Feel your lungs fill with air. Then, let your breath out through your mouth while you count from one to five. Take another deep breath and slowly let it out. If you breathe deeply enough, you will feel the hand on your stomach moving. Repeat this way of breathing several times. You'll be surprised at how much calmer you feel.

Learning how to breathe deeply may take a little work at first. But just keep in mind, "practice makes perfect."

3. Answer the QUESTIONS FOR PAIR B together.

QUESTIONS FOR PAIR B

  a. How do most people breathe when they are stressed?

  _____

  b. What kind of breathing helps the body relax?

  _____

  c. Describe the steps of deep breathing.

  _____

4. Find a Pair A with page 24. Ask them the QUESTIONS TO ASK PAIR A. Write their answers.

QUESTIONS TO ASK PAIR A

  a. When you practice visualization, what do you think about?

  _____

  b. What do you use all your senses to remember?

  _____

  c. What else do you do during visualization?

  _____

5. Answer Pair A's questions about your article.

KEEP GOING!
Talk about other relaxation strategies. What strategies work best for you?

Unit 1 Jigsaw Reading   25

What's Your Opinion?

The Project: Create a survey about learning
Supplies: notebook paper and pens, or use a word processing program (if computers are available)
Resources: dictionaries

Taking Tests Survey

1. Do you prefer written tests or oral tests?
2. Are tests helpful, or do they only make students nervous?
3.
4.

1. Work with 3–5 students. Introduce yourself.

2. Choose your job.

> **Leader:** Help your team work together and watch the time.
> **Recorder:** Write the team's ideas.
> **Supplier:** Get the supplies and the resources.
> **Researcher:** Find information to help your team complete the project.
> **Reporter:** Tell the class about the project.

3. As a team, choose a topic for your survey: learning English, learning materials (such as books, maps, and videos), study habits, taking tests, or another topic of your choice.

4. Brainstorm some *or* questions you can ask about the topic such as: Do you prefer English books or magazines?

> **Leader:** Give the team 5 minutes. Ask each person to suggest 1 question for the survey.
> **Recorder:** Write the name and the question of each team member.

5. Create the survey.

> **Supplier:** Get the supplies and the resources from your teacher.
> **Team:**
> • Write the topic at the top of the paper.
> • Write 4 *or* questions about your topic.
> • If possible, make copies of your survey for your classmates to complete.
> **Researcher:** Use a dictionary to help your team with vocabulary and spelling.

6. Show your project to the class

> **Reporter:** Ask another team to complete your survey. Give them a copy or read them the questions.

> **KEEP GOING!**
> After another team has completed your survey, look at their answers.
> Talk about the results with your team.

Unit 2 Keeping Current

Lesson 1: Picture Differences
Did You See Today's Paper?
Picture A 28
Picture B 29

Lesson 2: Round Table Writing 30
Who, What, Where, When, and Why?

Lesson 3
Peer Dictation: In the News 31
Survey: What Can You Remember? 32

Lesson 4: Role-Play 33
I Can Understand That

Lesson 5: Jigsaw Reading
Rescued by Their Pets!
Pair A 34
Pair B 35

Review and Expand
Team Project: Read All About It 36

Picture A: Did You See Today's Paper?

1. Find a partner with Picture B (page 29). Don't show this paper to your partner!

2. Work with your partner to find 10 differences between your pictures.

3. Write the picture differences in the chart below.

	Picture A	Picture B
1.	*The man is reading the editorial page.*	*The man is reading the classified ads.*
2.		
3.		
4.		
5.		
6.		
7.		
8.		
9.		
10.		

KEEP GOING!

Talk about the newspaper. What are your favorite sections? Why?

Picture B: Did You See Today's Paper?

1. Find a partner with Picture A (page 28). Don't show this paper to your partner!

2. Work with your partner to find 10 differences between your pictures.

3. Write the picture differences in the chart below.

	Picture A	Picture B
1.	*The man is reading the editorial page.*	*The man is reading the classified ads.*
2.		
3.		
4.		
5.		
6.		
7.		
8.		
9.		
10.		

KEEP GOING!

Talk about the newspaper. What are your favorite sections? Why?

Who, What, Where, When, and Why?

1. Work with 3 classmates.

2. Look at the pictures. Read the first sentence.

3. Brainstorm sentences about the pictures

4. Take turns writing sentences to continue the story.

5. Check your spelling in a dictionary.

One night last November, a crime took place in Merryvale City.

KEEP GOING!

Exchange stories with another group. What do you find interesting, surprising, or funny about their story?

In the News

Partner A
• **Read a sentence to Partner B.** • **Listen to Partner B repeat the sentence.**   **Is it correct? If not, say it again.**
1. A lot of money was stolen from the bank on Main Street. 2. Thousands of dollars were taken by the robber. 3. The robber was caught a few hours later. 4. The story was reported in yesterday's newspaper.
• **Listen to Partner B say a sentence.** • **Repeat the sentence.** • **Write the sentence.**
5.
6.
7.
8.

- - - - - - - - - - - - - - - -FOLD HERE- - - - - - - - - - - - - - - -

Partner B
• **Listen to Partner A say a sentence.** • **Repeat the sentence.** • **Write the sentence.**
1.
2.
3.
4.
• **Read a sentence to Partner A.** • **Listen to Partner A repeat the sentence.**   **Is it correct? If not, say it again.**
5. A baseball game was covered in the sports section. 6. The visiting team was expected to win. 7. The game was won by the home team. 8. A big celebration was held at a hotel in town.

KEEP GOING!

Write 5 sentences to describe real or imaginary events in the news.
Talk about the sentences with your partner.
A car was stolen from the parking lot on Maple Street.

What Can You Remember?

1. Read the questions. Write your answers in the chart.
2. Ask your classmates the questions in the chart.
3. Write your classmates' names and answers in the chart.
4. Use complete sentences to answer your classmates' questions.

Ask and answer these questions.	My answers	_____'s answers	_____'s answers	_____'s answers
What movie was recently shown at your local theater?				
What sports event was shown on TV recently?				
What important event was recently reported in the newspaper?				
Whose picture was seen on last week's front page?				
What song was recently played on the radio?				

5. Work with a partner. Compare your charts. Write 6 sentences.

Some students said that Star Games 2 was recently shown at their local theater.

1. _____
2. _____
3. _____
4. _____
5. _____
6. _____

KEEP GOING!

Can people learn more English by reading books and newspapers or by watching TV and movies? Talk about your opinions with the class.

I Can Understand That

1. Work with 3 classmates. Say all the lines in the script.
2. Choose your character.
3. Finish the conversation. Write more lines for each character.
4. Practice the lines.
5. Act out the role-play with your group.

Scene	Characters	Props
In front of a library	• Jo • Sam • Ari • Pat	A newspaper

The Script

Jo: Wow. Just look at this old library. What a great building!

Sam: There was a protest here yesterday. Did you read the news article about it?

Ari: No, I didn't. What was it about?

Sam: The city wants to remove the library and put up a building with four stories here.

Pat: The city wants to build four stores here?

Jo: No, a building with four stories.

Pat: Oh. So? What's wrong with that?

Sam: This library gives our city personality, and it's an important part of our history.

Jo: The protesters want to protect buildings like this.

Ari: I can understand that. It's good that citizens are expressing themselves.

Pat: So, what's going to happen to the old library?

KEEP GOING!

Watch your classmates' role-plays. Write the answers to these questions: What is going to happen to the old library? Do the friends agree or disagree with the decision?

Pair A: Rescued by Their Pets!

1. Find a partner with page 34. You are Pair A.

2. Read the article.

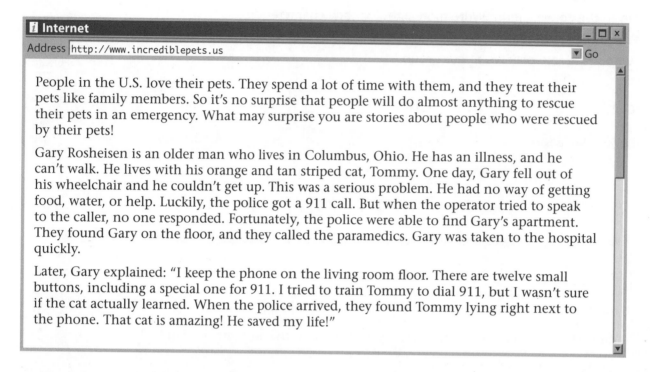

Internet

Address http://www.incrediblepets.us ▼ Go

People in the U.S. love their pets. They spend a lot of time with them, and they treat their pets like family members. So it's no surprise that people will do almost anything to rescue their pets in an emergency. What may surprise you are stories about people who were rescued by their pets!

Gary Rosheisen is an older man who lives in Columbus, Ohio. He has an illness, and he can't walk. He lives with his orange and tan striped cat, Tommy. One day, Gary fell out of his wheelchair and he couldn't get up. This was a serious problem. He had no way of getting food, water, or help. Luckily, the police got a 911 call. But when the operator tried to speak to the caller, no one responded. Fortunately, the police were able to find Gary's apartment. They found Gary on the floor, and they called the paramedics. Gary was taken to the hospital quickly.

Later, Gary explained: "I keep the phone on the living room floor. There are twelve small buttons, including a special one for 911. I tried to train Tommy to dial 911, but I wasn't sure if the cat actually learned. When the police arrived, they found Tommy lying right next to the phone. That cat is amazing! He saved my life!"

3. Answer the QUESTIONS FOR PAIR A together.

QUESTIONS FOR PAIR A

   a. Why did Gary need help?

   _____

   b. What happened when the operator tried to speak to the caller?

   _____

   c. How did Tommy help Gary?

   _____

4. Find a Pair B with page 35. Answer their questions about your article.

5. Ask them the QUESTIONS TO ASK PAIR B. Write their answers.

QUESTIONS TO ASK PAIR B

   a. What happened to Michael and Honey?

   _____

   b. How did Honey help Michael?

   _____

   c. How did Michael help Honey?

   _____

KEEP GOING!

Talk about pets. Did you or your friends ever have a pet that did something unusual?

Pair B: Rescued by Their Pets!

1. Find a partner with page 35. You are Pair B.

2. Read the article.

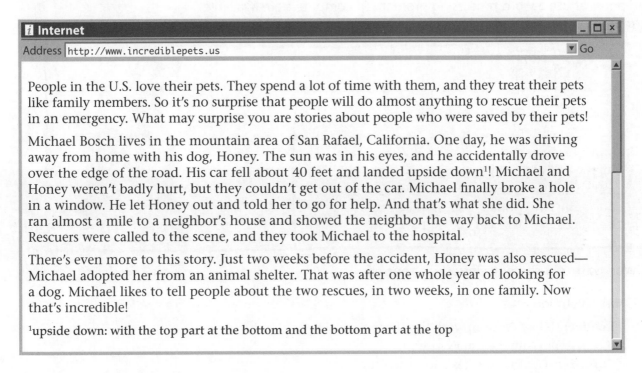

Internet

Address http://www.incrediblepets.us   ▼ Go

People in the U.S. love their pets. They spend a lot of time with them, and they treat their pets like family members. So it's no surprise that people will do almost anything to rescue their pets in an emergency. What may surprise you are stories about people who were saved by their pets!

Michael Bosch lives in the mountain area of San Rafael, California. One day, he was driving away from home with his dog, Honey. The sun was in his eyes, and he accidentally drove over the edge of the road. His car fell about 40 feet and landed upside down[1]! Michael and Honey weren't badly hurt, but they couldn't get out of the car. Michael finally broke a hole in a window. He let Honey out and told her to go for help. And that's what she did. She ran almost a mile to a neighbor's house and showed the neighbor the way back to Michael. Rescuers were called to the scene, and they took Michael to the hospital.

There's even more to this story. Just two weeks before the accident, Honey was also rescued—Michael adopted her from an animal shelter. That was after one whole year of looking for a dog. Michael likes to tell people about the two rescues, in two weeks, in one family. Now that's incredible!

[1]upside down: with the top part at the bottom and the bottom part at the top

3. Answer the QUESTIONS FOR PAIR B together.

QUESTIONS FOR PAIR B

    a. What happened to Michael and Honey?

    _____

    b. How did Honey help Michael?

    _____

    c. How did Michael help Honey?

    _____

4. Find a Pair A with page 34. Ask them the QUESTIONS TO ASK PAIR A. Write their answers.

QUESTIONS TO ASK PAIR A

    a. Why did Gary need help?

    _____

    b. What happened when the operator tried to speak to the caller?

    _____

    c. How did Tommy help Gary?

    _____

5. Answer Pair A's questions about your article.

KEEP GOING!
Talk about pets. Did you or your friends ever have a pet that did something unusual?

Read All About It

The Project: Create a section of a newspaper
Supplies: construction paper, newsprint or notebook paper, scissors, glue, colored markers, pencils and pens, or use a word processing program (if computers are available)
Resources: magazines or information from the Internet, dictionaries

SPORTS

Local Team Wins!

Last night, the Glengate women's soccer team played an exciting game against Hillsville. With 5 minutes left in the game, Linda Gomez made the winning goal. Final score: Glengate 2, Hillsville 1.

1. Work with 3–5 students. Introduce yourself.

2. Choose your job.

> **Leader:** Help your team work together and watch the time.
> **Recorder:** Write the team's ideas.
> **Supplier:** Get the supplies and the resources.
> **Researcher:** Find information to help your team complete the project.
> **Reporter:** Tell the class about the project.

3. As a team, choose a topic for your newspaper section: Entertainment, International News, Local News, Sports, or another section of your choice.

> **Leader:** Give the team 10 minutes. Ask each person for ideas for different topics.
> **Recorder:** Write the name and ideas of each team member.
> **Team:** Choose 2-3 topics to write about.
> **Researcher:** Find more information about the topics for your section. Talk about the information with your team.

4. Write the section.

> **Supplier:** Get the supplies and the resources from your teacher.
> **Team:**
> • Write the articles for your section. Give each article a headline.
> • Find or draw pictures to go with your articles.
> • Help the Reporter choose an article for a class presentation.

5. Show your project to the class.

> **Reporter:** Talk about the most interesting article in your section.

KEEP GOING!
Put all the teams' sections together to create a class newspaper.

Unit 3 Going Places

Lesson 1: Picture Differences
Car Trouble!
Picture A 38
Picture B 39

Lesson 2: Round Table Writing 40
Would You Like to Leave a Message?

Lesson 3
Peer Dictation: What Did They Say? 41
Survey: What Did You Say? 42

Lesson 4: Role-Play 43
Why Don't You Drive There?

Lesson 5: Jigsaw Reading
Telephones of Tomorrow
Pair A 44
Pair B 45

Review and Expand
Team Project: The Latest Thing for Travelers 46

Picture A: Car Trouble!

1. Find a partner with Picture B (page 39). Don't show this paper to your partner!

2. Work with your partner to find 10 differences between your pictures.

3. Write the picture differences in the chart below.

	Picture A	Picture B
1.	*The truck had a breakdown.*	*The car had a breakdown.*
2.		
3.		
4.		
5.		
6.		
7.		
8.		
9.		
10.		

KEEP GOING!
Talk about transportation. Do you prefer driving or using public transportation? Why?

Picture B: Car Trouble!

1. Find a partner with Picture A (page 38). Don't show this paper to your partner!

2. Work with your partner to find 10 differences between your pictures.

3. Write the picture differences in the chart below.

	Picture A	Picture B
1.	*The truck had a breakdown.*	*The car had a breakdown.*
2.		
3.		
4.		
5.		
6.		
7.		
8.		
9.		
10.		

KEEP GOING!
Talk about transportation. Do you prefer driving or using public transportation? Why?

Would You Like to Leave a Message?

1. Work with 3 classmates.
2. Look at the pictures. Read the first sentence.
3. Brainstorm sentences about the pictures.
4. Take turns writing sentences to continue the story.
5. Check your spelling in a dictionary.

Using English on the phone was very difficult for Lucy.

_____

_____

_____

_____

_____

_____

_____

_____

KEEP GOING!

Exchange stories with another group. What do you find interesting, surprising, or funny about their story?

What Did They Say?

Partner A
• **Read a sentence to Partner B.**   • **Listen to Partner B repeat the sentence.**   **Is it correct? If not, say it again.**
1. My friends called and said they were stuck in traffic.   2. They said, "We're sorry, but we're going to be late."   3. I told them that it wasn't a problem.   4. I said, "I'll definitely wait for you."
• **Listen to Partner B say a sentence.**   • **Repeat the sentence.**   • **Write the sentence.**
5.
6.
7.
8.

- FOLD HERE -

Partner B
• **Listen to Partner A say a sentence.**   • **Repeat the sentence.**   • **Write the sentence.**
1.
2.
3.
4.
• **Read a sentence to Partner A.**   • **Listen to Partner A repeat the sentence.**   **Is it correct? If not, say it again.**
5. Nancy called and said, "I'm having car problems."   6. She told me that she was locked out of her car.   7. I said, "I'm sorry, but I don't think I can help you."   8. I told her that she needed to call the auto club.

KEEP GOING!

Write 5 sentences to report what someone said in class today.
Talk about the sentences with your partner.
Ted told me he woke up late this morning.

What Did You Say?

1. Read the questions. Write your answers in the chart.
2. Ask your classmates the questions in the chart.
3. Write your classmates' names and answers in the chart.
4. Use complete sentences to answer your classmates' questions.

What did you say the last time…	My answers	_____'s answers	_____'s answers	_____'s answers
you heard a cell phone ring in a classroom?				
you heard someone talking during a movie?				
you couldn't understand someone on the phone?				
you called a wrong number?				
you came to school late?				
you were caught in the rain without an umbrella?				

5. Work with a partner. Compare your charts. Write 6 sentences.

   Most students said, "Please turn off your cell phone."

   1. _____
   2. _____
   3. _____
   4. _____
   5. _____
   6. _____

KEEP GOING!

Which answers to the questions were the funniest? Talk about your opinions with the class.

Why Don't You Drive There?

1. Work with 3 classmates. Say all the lines in the script.
2. Choose your character.
3. Finish the conversation. Write more lines for each character.
4. Practice the lines.
5. Act out the role-play with your group.

Scene	Characters	Props
After class	• Kim • Alex • Jan • Sasha	• Books • A pen • A piece of paper

The Script

Kim: What are you going to do during the school break?

Alex: Sasha and I are going to fly to Boston. We've never been there before.

Jan: Did you buy your tickets yet?

Sasha: Not yet. My friend told me to look for tickets on the Internet.

Jan: If I were you, I'd try TRIPS.us. I bet you can find some good prices there.

Sasha: That's a good idea. I should write that down. What's the website?

Jan: It's T – R – I – P – S – dot - U – S.

Kim: Why don't you drive to Boston?

Alex: That sounds like fun! But we'll need to get directions.

Sasha: That's true. Last year, when we tried to drive to Florida, we found ourselves in Mexico!

Jan: How about trying a map website?

KEEP GOING!

Watch your classmates' role-plays. Write the answers to these questions: Does Sasha decide to look for plane tickets or maps on the Internet? How are Sasha and Alex going to travel to Boston?

Pair A: Telephones of Tomorrow

1. Find a partner with page 44. You are Pair A.

2. Read the article.

Telephones have come a long way since the first phone of 1876. Today we only see the big, heavy phones of the past in museums or movies. In the "old days," most people didn't have a telephone at home. They had to go into town to make or receive a call. Just think how different this is from our world of cell phones today!

Today cell phones can do all kinds of things. For example, your cell can be a pocket-sized entertainment center. Many cell phones already have cameras and video games. But soon more people will have phones that allow them to watch TV, listen to music, and get Internet information. And that's not all! You probably won't need your wallet to shop or pay for movies, concerts, or restaurant meals. You'll be able to use your cell phone to pay for anything from a cup of coffee to a fancy coffee maker. In some countries, this is already true. You also won't need to carry car keys. You'll be able to start your car with a button on your phone. And when you're ready to return home, another button will open your garage door for you!

Who knows what else phones will do in the future? But one thing is sure. You won't want to leave home without yours!

3. Answer the QUESTIONS FOR PAIR A together.

QUESTIONS FOR PAIR A

   a. In what ways can a cell phone be an entertainment center?

    _____

   b. Why won't you need your wallet in the future?

    _____

   c. What else will you be able to do with your cell phone?

    _____

4. Find a Pair B with page 45. Answer their questions about your article.

5. Ask them the QUESTIONS FOR PAIR B. Write their answers.

QUESTIONS TO ASK PAIR B

   a. In what ways can a cell phone be like a personal assistant?

    _____

   b. What personal information will you be able to keep on your cell phone?

    _____

   c. Why won't you have to worry about losing your cell phones?

    _____

KEEP GOING!

Talk about the telephone. Have the changes in telephone technology always improved our lives? Why or why not?

Pair B: Telephones of Tomorrow

1. Find a partner with page 45. You are Pair B.

2. Read the article.

Telephones have come a long way since the first phone of 1876. Today we only see the big, heavy phones of the past in museums or movies. In the "old days," most people didn't have a telephone at home. They had to go into town to make or receive a call. Just think how different this is from our world of cell phones today!

Today cell phones can do all kinds of things. A cell phone can even be like a personal assistant. Some cell phones can now provide schedules for buses and trains, and planes may be next. A phone like this could help you make all your travel plans! Soon you may have a phone that reminds you about appointments and the due dates of your bills. Instead of mailing payments, you'll be able to make electronic payments with your phone. And that's not all. Researchers are working on cell phones that can keep your medical history on file, including your blood type, medications, and allergies. How convenient! And you won't have to worry about losing a cell phone with all your personal information. You'll have a personal identification code for your phone, so it won't work for anyone but you.

Who knows what else phones will do in the future? But one thing is sure. You won't want to leave home without yours!

3. Answer the QUESTIONS FOR PAIR B together.

QUESTIONS FOR PAIR B

    a. In what ways can a cell phone be like a personal assistant?

_____

    b. What personal information will you be able to keep on your cell phone?

_____

    c. Why won't you have to worry about losing your cell phone?

_____

4. Find a Pair A with page 44. Ask them the QUESTIONS FOR PAIR A. Write their answers.

QUESTIONS TO ASK PAIR A

    a. In what ways is a cell phone like an entertainment center?

_____

    b. Why won't you need your wallet in the future?

_____

    c. What else will you be able to do with your cell phone?

_____

5. Answer Pair A's questions about your article.

KEEP GOING!

Talk about the telephone. Have the changes in telephone technology always improved our lives? Why or why not?

The Latest Thing for Travelers

The Project: Create an ad for a new travel product
Supplies: poster board, markers, colored pencils or crayons, pens
Resources: dictionaries

Your coffee stays hot to the bottom of the cup!

THE HOT CUP

Are you tired of drinking cold coffee? Take the Hot Cup on your next trip. It will keep your coffee hot for hours!

190°F

1. Work with 3–5 students. Introduce yourself.

2. Choose your job.

> **Leader:** Help your team work together and watch the time.
> **Recorder:** Write the team's ideas.
> **Supplier:** Get the supplies and the resources.
> **Graphic Designer:** Design the ad and draw a picture for your team's project.
> **Researcher:** Find information to help your teammates complete the project.
> **Reporter:** Tell the class about the project.

3. Brainstorm ideas for a new travel product.

> **Leader:** Give the team 10 minutes. Ask each person for one idea.
> **Recorder:** Write the name and ideas of each team member.

4. Choose one product and create the ad.

> **Supplier:** Get the supplies and the resources from your teacher.
> **Team:**
> • Decide on a product, and write its name on the ad.
> • Write a short sentence to help sell the product.
> • Write a paragraph describing what the product does. Include a picture of the product.
> **Graphic Designer:** Help your team design an attractive ad.
> **Researcher:** Use a dictionary to help your team with vocabulary and spelling.

5. Show your project to the class.

> **Reporter:** Describe your team's product. Tell what makes it special.

KEEP GOING!

After all the teams have presented their ads, vote on which travel product is the best.

Unit 4 Get the Job

Lesson 1: Picture Differences
Steps to a Career
Picture A 48
Picture B 49

Lesson 2: Round Table Writing 50
Job Skills to Go!

Lesson 3
Peer Dictation: What Had They Done? 51
Survey: I Had Never Learned That Before 52

Lesson 4: Role-Play 53
Have You Had Any Training?

Lesson 5: Jigsaw Reading
Make or Break Your Next Interview!
Pair A 54
Pair B 55

Review and Expand
Team Project: The Right Person for the Right Job 56

Picture A: Steps to a Career

1. Find a partner with Picture B (page 49). Don't show this paper to your partner!

2. Work with your partner to find 10 differences between your pictures.

3. Write the picture differences in the chart below.

	Picture A	Picture B
1.	*The man is taking an interest inventory.*	*The man is applying for financial aid.*
2.		
3.		
4.		
5.		
6.		
7.		
8.		
9.		
10.		

KEEP GOING!

Talk about career planning. What are the three most important things you can do to prepare for a career?

Picture B: Steps to a Career

1. Find a partner with Picture A (page 48). Don't show this paper to your partner!

2. Work with your partner to find 10 differences between your pictures.

3. Write the picture differences in the chart below.

	Picture A	Picture B
1.	*The man is taking an interest inventory.*	*The man is applying for financial aid.*
2.		
3.		
4.		
5.		
6.		
7.		
8.		
9.		
10.		

KEEP GOING!

Talk about career planning. What are the three most important things you can do to prepare for a career?

Job Skills to Go!

1. Work with 3 classmates.
2. Look at the pictures. Read the first sentence.
3. Brainstorm sentences about the pictures.
4. Take turns writing sentences to continue the story.
5. Check your spelling in a dictionary.

Elena Ramirez is ready to change jobs, but she's learned a lot of skills in this one.

_____

_____

_____

_____

_____

_____

_____

KEEP GOING!

Exchange stories with another group. What do you find interesting, surprising, or funny about their story?

What Had They Done?

Partner A
• **Read a sentence to Partner B.** • **Listen to Partner B repeat the sentence.**   **Is it correct? If not, say it again.**
1. Ben had studied beginning English before he came to the U.S. 2. He continued to study here in a higher level class. 3. Sara had never studied English before. 4. She needed to start in a beginning English class.
• **Listen to Partner B say a sentence.** • **Repeat the sentence.** • **Write the sentence.**
5.
6.
7.
8.

- -Fold Here- - - - - - - - - - - - - - - -

Partner B
• **Listen to Partner A say a sentence.** • **Repeat the sentence.** • **Write the sentence.**
1.
2.
3.
4.
• **Read a sentence to Partner A.** • **Listen to Partner A repeat the sentence.**   **Is it correct? If not, say it again.**
5. What had Carlos done before he came to the U.S.? 6. He had worked as an auto mechanic in his country. 7. He had taken several training classes, too. 8. He got a good job here as a mechanic at a garage in town.

KEEP GOING!

Write 5 sentences to describe your experiences before you came to this school.
I had studied English in China before I came to this school.

I Had Never Learned That Before

1. Read the questions. Write your answers in the chart.
2. Ask your classmates the questions in the chart.
3. Write your classmates' names and answers in the chart.
4. Use complete sentences to answer your classmates' questions.

Ask and answer these questions.	My answers	_____'s answers	_____'s answers	_____'s answers
How many years had you studied English before this class?				
Had you studied other languages before you studied English?				
Had you thought about career planning before this class?				
Had you learned the past perfect before this class?				
What is something you had never learned before this class?				

5. Work with a partner. Compare your charts. Write 6 sentences.

Most students had studied English for two years before this class.

1. _____
2. _____
3. _____
4. _____
5. _____
6. _____

KEEP GOING!

What is one topic you had never discussed before this class?
Talk about your ideas with the class.

Have You Had Any Training?

1. Work with 2 classmates. Say all the lines in the script.
2. Choose your character.
3. Finish the conversation. Write more lines for each character.
4. Practice the lines.
5. Act out the role-play with your group.

Scene	Characters	Props
An office	• Personnel Manager • Applicant • Sales Manager	• Three chairs • Notepads or paper • Pens

The Script

Personnel Manager: Thanks for coming today. We really liked your cover letter.

Applicant: Oh, thank you for saying so.

Sales Manager: So, how did you learn about the position? Did someone tell you about it?

Applicant: Actually, no. I read about it in the classified ads.

Personnel Manager: Had you heard of our company before that?

Applicant: Yes. I've done a lot of research on clothing companies.

Sales Manager: What kind of training have you had?

Applicant: Do you mean sales training?

Personnel Manager: Yes, and any other training, too.

Applicant: Well, I had two months of on-the-job training at Suit-2-Boot.

Sales Manager: Good. Tell me, do you like your current job?

KEEP GOING!
Watch your classmates' role-plays. Write the answers to these questions: What does the applicant say about his or her current job? Does the applicant get the job?

Pair A: Make or Break Your Next Interview!

1. Find a partner with page 54. You are Pair A.

2. Read the article.

Employment Weekly: People often say, "First impressions last." That's true. We form opinions about people when we first meet them, and those opinions don't usually change. No one knows this better than Ms. Gina Goodjob. She's been a personnel manager for over 20 years. We recently talked to Gina about her best-selling book, *Make or Break Your Next Interview.*

EW: Gina, you wrote a lot about "interview makers." What are they?

Gina: Interview makers are the things you can do to help an interview go well. For example, Learn about the company before your interview. This will show the employer that you are interested. Give yourself a pep talk, too. Tell yourself you *can* get the job.

A positive attitude will help the interviewer take more interest in you.

EW: There's a chapter in your book on being prepared. What is that about?

Gina: That's very important. Be prepared to discuss your strengths and the areas you want to improve. Be ready to explain why you want the job. Plan to talk about your experiences in a positive way, even if your last job was terrible.

EW: What about after the interview?

Gina: Send the interviewer a thank you note—that's a sure interview maker. OK, that's enough for today. If you want more advice, you'll have to buy my book!

3. Answer the QUESTIONS FOR PAIR A together.

QUESTIONS FOR PAIR A

   a. What is an "interview maker"?

_____

   b. What are two interview makers to think about before an interview?

_____

   c. What is an important interview maker to remember after an interview?

_____

4. Find a Pair B with page 55. Answer their questions about your article.

5. Ask them the QUESTIONS TO ASK PAIR B. Write their answers.

QUESTIONS TO ASK PAIR B

   a. What is an "interview breaker"?

_____

   b. What is one interview breaker that can happen before an interview begins?

_____

   c. What are two other examples of interview breakers?

_____

> **KEEP GOING!**
> Talk about interviews. Do you think you make a good first impression? Why or why not?

Pair B: Make or Break Your Next Interview!

1. Find a partner with page 55. You are Pair B.

2. Read the article.

Employment Weekly: People often say, "First impressions last." That's true. We form opinions about people when we first meet them, and those opinions don't usually change. No one knows this better than Ms. Gina Goodjob. She's been a personnel manager for over 20 years. We recently talked to Gina about her best-selling book, *Make or Break Your Next Interview.*

EW: Gina, you wrote a lot about "interview breakers." What are they?

Gina: Interview breakers are the mistakes you need to avoid. Interview breakers almost guarantee you won't get hired. Sometimes they happen before an interview even begins. Don't be late—that's the worst! Employers will think it's your habit. Know where you're going and allow plenty of time to get there.

EW: Are there interview breakers to remember during the interview?

Gina: Yes. Don't be dishonest about your experience. If you can't tell the truth, then you're probably not the right person for the job. Don't talk too much either. Don't let your answers go on and on. You'll make a better impression with focused, clear answers. Think about quality, not quantity.

EW: Is there anything else we should know?

Gina: Don't leave your cell phone on—that's a sure interview breaker! OK, that's enough for today. If you want more advice, you'll have to buy my book!

3. Answer the QUESTIONS FOR PAIR B together.

QUESTIONS FOR PAIR B

a. What is an "interview breaker"?

_____

b. What is one interview breaker that can happen before an interview begins?

_____

c. What are two other examples of interview breakers?

_____

4. Find a Pair A with page 54. Ask them the QUESTIONS TO ASK PAIR A. Write their answers.

QUESTIONS TO ASK PAIR A

a. What is an "interview maker"?

_____

b. What are two interview makers to think about before an interview?

_____

c. What is an important interview maker to remember after an interview?

_____

5. Answer Pair A's questions about your article.

KEEP GOING!

Talk about job interviews. Do you think you make a good impression on the interviewer? Why or why not?

The Right Person for the Right Job

The Project: Find a job ad and write a description of the right person for the job
Supplies: chart paper, tape, colored markers, pencils and pens, or use a word processing program (if computers are available)
Resources: dictionaries, classified ads section of newspapers

— Help Wanted — DELIVERY PERSON Busy Delivery Co. F/T, M-F, License Req. Must know area Call (205) 555-9945	*The right person* • *is a good driver.* • *has a driver's license.* • *is efficient.* • *knows the neighborhood.*

1. Work with 3–5 students. Introduce yourself.

2. Choose your job.

> **Leader:** Help your team work together and watch the time.
> **Recorder:** Write the team's ideas.
> **Supplier:** Get the supplies and the resources.
> **Researcher:** Find information to help your teammates complete the project.
> **Reporter:** Tell the class about the project.

3. As a team, choose a job ad from the classified section of a newspaper.

> **Supplier:** Get the supplies and the resources from your teacher.
> **Team:** Choose a job ad. Talk about the ad with your team. Discuss the abbreviations.

4. Brainstorm ideas about the skills, experience, and personal qualities needed for this job.

> **Leader:** Give the team 5 minutes. Ask each person for ideas.
> **Recorder:** Write the name and ideas of each team member.

5. Write the description.

> **Team:**
> • Cut out the job ad and put it at the top of the paper.
> • Write a description of the right person for the job.
> **Researcher:** Use a dictionary to help your team with vocabulary and spelling.

6. Show your project to the class.

> **Reporter:** Describe the job in the ad. Talk about the qualifications of the right person for this job.

KEEP GOING!

Are you the right person for any of the jobs in the ads?
Talk about your answer with the class.

Unit 5 Safe and Sound

Lesson 1: Picture Differences
Use Caution!
Picture A...58
Picture B...59

Lesson 2: Round Table Writing.......................................60
It's Good to Be Prepared

Lesson 3
Peer Dictation: Be Careful, Be Prepared 61
Survey: Things You've Got to Do.......................................62

Lesson 4: Role-Play...63
I'd Like to Report a Safety Hazard

Lesson 5: Jigsaw Reading
What Do You Know About Home Safety?
Pair A 64
Pair B 65

Review and Expand
Team Project: Safety Survey...66

Picture A: Use Caution!

1. Find a partner with Picture B (page 59). Don't show this paper to your partner!

2. Work with your partner to find 10 differences between your pictures.

3. Write the picture differences in the chart below.

	Picture A	Picture B
1.	*The corrosive chemicals are on a shelf.*	*The flammable liquids are on a shelf.*
2.		
3.		
4.		
5.		
6.		
7.		
8.		
9.		
10.		

KEEP GOING!

Talk about safety hazards. What was the last safety hazard you saw?
What did you do about it?

Picture B: Use Caution!

1. Find a partner with Picture A (page 58). Don't show this paper to your partner!

2. Work with your partner to find 10 differences between your pictures.

3. Write the picture differences in the chart below.

	Picture A	**Picture B**
1.	*The corrosive chemicals are on a shelf.*	*The flammable liquids are on a shelf.*
2.		
3.		
4.		
5.		
6.		
7.		
8.		
9.		
10.		

KEEP GOING!

Talk about safety hazards. What was the last safety hazard you saw?
What did you do about it?

It's Good to Be Prepared

1. Work with 3 classmates.
2. Look at the pictures. Read the first sentence.
3. Brainstorm sentences about the pictures.
4. Take turns writing sentences to continue the story.
5. Check your spelling in a dictionary.

Last week the Ramos family made their emergency plan, and it was a good thing they did.

_____

_____

_____

_____

_____

_____

_____

_____

KEEP GOING!

Exchange stories with another group. What do you find interesting, surprising, or funny about their story?

Be Careful, Be Prepared

Partner A
• **Read a sentence to Partner B.** • **Listen to Partner B repeat the sentence.**   **Is it correct? If not, say it again.**
1. We've got to read the warning labels on flammable liquids. 2. We must not use them near an open fire. 3. You don't have to be nervous about using them. 4. I'm just saying we have to be careful.
• **Listen to Partner B say a sentence.** • **Repeat the sentence.** • **Write the sentence.**
5.
6.
7.
8.

- - - - - - - - - - - - - - - FOLD HERE- - - - - - - - - - - - - - -

Partner B
• **Listen to Partner A say a sentence.** • **Repeat the sentence.** • **Write the sentence.**
1.
2.
3.
4.
• **Read a sentence to Partner A.** • **Listen to Partner A repeat the sentence.**   **Is it correct? If not, say it again.**
5. My family had to make an emergency plan. 6. I had to buy a lot of emergency supplies. 7. I didn't have to buy a first-aid kit or bottled water. 8. We already had those at home.

KEEP GOING!

Work with your partner. Write 5 sentences to give safety advice.
You must wear safety gloves when you work with corrosive chemicals.

Things You've Got to Do

1. Read the questions. Write your answers in the chart.

2. Ask your classmates the questions in the chart.

3. Write your classmates' names and answers in the chart.

4. Use complete sentences to answer your classmates' questions.

What is one thing . . .	My answers	_____'s answers	_____'s answers	_____'s answers
you always have to carry with you?				
all drivers have to keep in their cars?				
you must buy for your emergency kit?				
you must do before using dangerous chemicals?				
you've got to fix at home?				

5. Work with a partner. Compare your charts. Write 6 sentences.

Many students think that everyone has to carry identification.

1. _____

2. _____

3. _____

4. _____

5. _____

6. _____

KEEP GOING!

Are you prepared for an emergency at home? Why or why not? Talk about your opinions with the class.

I'd Like to Report a Safety Hazard

1. Work with 2 classmates. Say all the lines in the script.

2. Choose your character.

3. Finish the conversation. Write more lines for each character.

4. Practice the lines.

5. Act out the role-play with your group.

Scene	Characters	Props
An office	• Employee • Manager • Safety Supervisor	2 telephones

The Script

Employee: Excuse me, sir. I'd like to report a safety hazard.

Manager: What seems to be the problem?

Employee: I noticed there aren't any fire extinguishers on this floor.

Manager: Thanks for letting me know. I'll call the safety supervisor.

Safety Supervisor: Safety Department. This is Pat Jones speaking.

Manager: This is the first floor manager. Our fire extinguishers are gone.

Safety Supervisor: Really? The workers should have replaced those old extinguishers with new ones.

Manager: We've got to have those new extinguishers as soon as possible.

Safety Supervisor: Thanks for reporting the problem. I'll take care of it right away.

Employee: Uh...excuse me, there's another problem, too.

KEEP GOING!

Watch your classmates' role-plays. Write the answers to these questions:
What other safety hazard did the employee report? What did the manager say?

Pair A: What Do You Know About Home Safety?

1. Find a partner with page 64. You are Pair A.

2. Read the article.

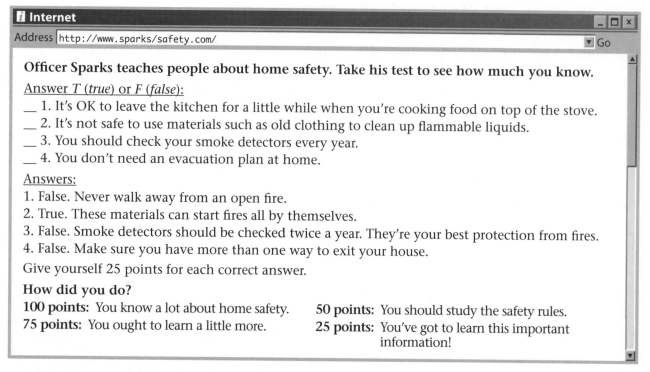

3. Answer the QUESTIONS FOR PAIR A together.

QUESTIONS FOR PAIR A

a. Why should you never leave the kitchen while you are cooking?

_____

b. Why are smoke detectors so important?

_____

c. What should you think about when you make an evacuation plan?

_____

4. Find a Pair B with page 65. Answer their questions about your article.

5. Ask them the QUESTIONS TO ASK PAIR B. Write their answers.

QUESTIONS TO ASK PAIR B

a. What shouldn't you do if an electrical item falls in the water?

_____

b. Why shouldn't you put electrical cords under rugs or furniture?

_____

c. When is it OK to use a repaired electrical cord?

_____

KEEP GOING!

Talk about safety. What are some safety rules that people sometimes don't follow?

Pair B: What Do You Know About Home Safety?

1. Find a partner with page 65. You are Pair B.

2. Read the article.

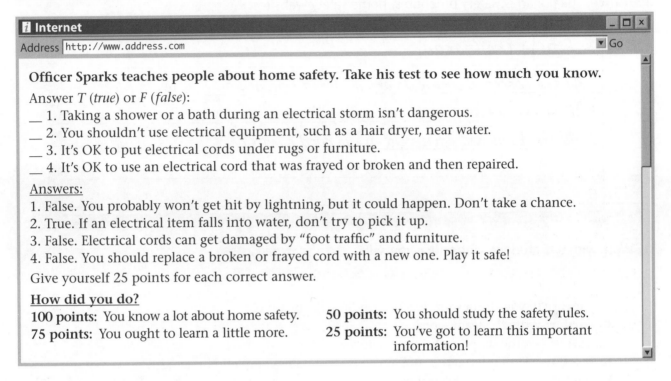

Officer Sparks teaches people about home safety. Take his test to see how much you know.

Answer *T* (*true*) or *F* (*false*):

__ 1. Taking a shower or a bath during an electrical storm isn't dangerous.
__ 2. You shouldn't use electrical equipment, such as a hair dryer, near water.
__ 3. It's OK to put electrical cords under rugs or furniture.
__ 4. It's OK to use an electrical cord that was frayed or broken and then repaired.

<u>Answers:</u>
1. False. You probably won't get hit by lightning, but it could happen. Don't take a chance.
2. True. If an electrical item falls into water, don't try to pick it up.
3. False. Electrical cords can get damaged by "foot traffic" and furniture.
4. False. You should replace a broken or frayed cord with a new one. Play it safe!

Give yourself 25 points for each correct answer.

<u>How did you do?</u>
100 points: You know a lot about home safety.   **50 points:** You should study the safety rules.
75 points: You ought to learn a little more.   **25 points:** You've got to learn this important information!

3. Answer the QUESTIONS FOR PAIR B together.

QUESTIONS FOR PAIR B

   a. What shouldn't you do if an electrical item falls into water?

   _____

   b. Why shouldn't you put electrical cords under rugs or furniture?

   _____

   c. When is it OK to use a repaired electrical cord?

   _____

4. Find a Pair A with page 64. Ask them the QUESTIONS TO ASK PAIR A. Write their answers.

QUESTIONS TO ASK PAIR A

   a. Why should you never leave the kitchen while you are cooking?

   _____

   b. Why are smoke detectors so important?

   _____

   c. What should you think about when you make an evacuation plan?

   _____

5. Answer Pair A's questions about your article.

KEEP GOING!

Talk about safety. What are some safety rules that people sometimes don't follow?

Safety Survey

The Project: Create a survey about home safety
Supplies: notebook paper and pens, or use a word processing program (if computers are available)
Resources: dictionaries, safety brochures, home safety websites

	Safety in the Garage		
○	1. All the corrosive chemicals are in closed containers.	Yes	No
	2. There are safety glasses and safety gloves.	Yes	No
	3. All the tools and equipment are in good condition.	Yes	No
	4.		
	5.		

1. Work with 3–5 students. Introduce yourself.

2. Choose your job.

> **Leader:** Help your team work together and watch the time.
> **Recorder:** Write the team's ideas.
> **Supplier:** Get the supplies and the resources.
> **Researcher:** Find information to help your teammates complete the project.
> **Reporter:** Tell the class about the project.

3. As a team, choose a place for your home safety survey: bathroom, bedroom, kitchen, living room, garage, or another place of your choice.

4. Brainstorm safety features for your place.

> **Leader:** Give the team 5 minutes. Ask each person for ideas.
> **Recorder:** Write the name and ideas of each team member.

5. Create the survey.

> **Supplier:** Get the supplies and the resources from your teacher.
> **Team:**
> • Write 5-10 sentences about safety in your place.
> • Number the sentences and write *Yes* and *No* next to each one.
> • If possible, make copies of your team's survey for your classmates.
> **Researcher:** Use a dictionary to help your team with vocabulary and spelling.

6. Show your project to the class.

> **Reporter:** Ask another team to complete your survey. You can read the questions or give them a copy.

KEEP GOING!

After another team has completed your survey, look at their answers.
Talk about the results with your team.

Unit 6 Getting Ahead

Lesson 1: Picture Differences
Special Skills Make Special People
Picture A 68
Picture B 69

Lesson 2: Round Table Writing 70
Employee of the Month

Lesson 3
Peer Dictation: The Best Employees 71
Survey: Interpersonal Skills 72

Lesson 4: Role-Play 73
Who Do I Talk To?

Lesson 5: Jigsaw Reading
Dealing with Difficult Co-workers
Pair A 74
Pair B 75

Review and Expand
Team Project: Know What to Do and Say 76

Picture A: Special Skills Make Special People

1. Find a partner with Picture B (page 69). Don't show this paper to your partner!

2. Work with your partner to find 10 differences between your pictures.

3. Write the picture differences in the chart below.

	Picture A	**Picture B**
1.	*The coach is making a suggestion.*	*The coach is managing conflict.*
2.		
3.		
4.		
5.		
6.		
7.		
8.		
9.		
10.		

KEEP GOING!

Talk about interpersonal skills. Which are the most important skills for team sports?

Picture B: Special Skills Make Special People

1. Find a partner with Picture A (page 68). Don't show this paper to your partner!
2. Work with your partner to find 10 differences between your pictures.

3. Write the picture differences in the chart below.

	Picture A	Picture B
1.	*The coach is making a suggestion.*	*The coach is managing conflict.*
2.		
3.		
4.		
5.		
6.		
7.		
8.		
9.		
10.		

KEEP GOING!

Talk about interpersonal skills. Which are the most important skills for team sports?

Employee of the Month

1. Work with 3 classmates.

2. Look at the pictures. Read the first sentence.

3. Brainstorm sentences about the pictures.

4. Take turns writing sentences to continue the story.

5. Check your spelling in a dictionary.

Today Genevieve Bastien got an award for showing the qualities and skills of an excellent employee.

_____

_____

_____

_____

_____

_____

_____

KEEP GOING!

Exchange stories with another group. What do you find interesting, surprising, or funny about their story?

The Best Employees

Partner A
• **Read a sentence to Partner B.** • **Listen to Partner B repeat the sentence.**   **Is it correct? If not, say it again.**
1. I read an article that describes the best employees. 2. I learned about skills that are important on the job. 3. Employers like employees who solve problems. 4. They don't like employees who create them.
• **Listen to Partner B say a sentence.** • **Repeat the sentence.** • **Write the sentence.**
5.
6.
7.
8.

- - - - - - - - - - - - - - - - - - -FOLD HERE- -

Partner B
• **Listen to Partner A say a sentence.** • **Repeat the sentence.** • **Write the sentence.**
1.
2.
3.
4.
• **Read a sentence to Partner A.** • **Listen to Partner A repeat the sentence.**   **Is it correct? If not, say it again.**
5. The company I work for gives awards to the best employees. 6. The name of the award they give is "Employee of the Week." 7. The manager who recommended me is my supervisor. 8. I'm the employee who won the award this week!

KEEP GOING!

Work with your partner. Write 5 sentences to describe people
or things at school or work.
The student who sits next to me is from Puerto Rico.

Interpersonal Skills

1. Read the questions. Write your answers in the chart.
2. Ask your classmates the questions in the chart.
3. Write your classmates' names and answers in the chart.
4. Use complete sentences to answer your classmates' questions.

Ask and answer these questions.	My answers	_____'s answers	_____'s answers	_____'s answers
Are you a person who responds well to feedback?				
Are you someone who can solve problems easily?				
What is one personal quality that is important in a friend?				
What is one interpersonal skill which is important at a job interview?				
What is one interpersonal skill that you'd like to work on?				

5. Work with a partner. Compare your charts. Write 6 sentences.

   Some students don't respond well to feedback.

1. _____
2. _____
3. _____
4. _____
5. _____
6. _____

KEEP GOING!

What are some ways to develop an interpersonal skill that you don't already have?
Talk about your opinions with the class.

Who Do I Talk To?

1. Work with 2 classmates. Say all the lines in the script.
2. Choose your character.
3. Finish the conversation. Write more lines for each character.
4. Practice the lines.
5. Act out the role-play with your group.

Scene 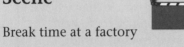 Break time at a factory	**Characters** • Co-worker 1 • Co-worker 2 • Co-worker 3	**Props** A piece of paper

The Script

Co-worker 1: Hi, there. How is your first day on the job going?

Co-worker 2: Not very well. I'm a little worried.

Co-worker 3: Really? What's the problem?

Co-worker 2: It's this work schedule. I can't work on Saturday. I have another job on weekends.

Co-worker 1: Relax! It's no problem. Who's your supervisor?

Co-worker 2: It's Ms. Crab. Should I talk to her?

Co-worker 3: No. You should talk to Mr. Kind, the Human Resources supervisor.

Co-worker 2: He's not the person who hired me. Where can I find him? What should I say?

KEEP GOING!

Watch your classmates' role-plays. Write the answers to these questions:
Where can Co-worker 2 find Mr. Kind? What should Co-worker 2 say to Mr. Kind?

Pair A: Dealing with Difficult Co-workers

1. Find a partner with page 74. You are Pair A.

2. Read the article.

Dr. Harry Hartley writes a popular advice column in the *Miami Star* about dealing with problems at work. Here is a letter he received from one reader last week, along with his advice.

Dear Dr. Hartley,

I'm having a hard time with one of my co-workers. Every time I ask her to help me, she says, "It's not *my* job." So I always have to do all the work myself. She's not a team player. What should I do?

  Annoyed

Dear Annoyed,

You're not alone. This is a very common problem. Employees often say, "It's not my job" to avoid doing extra work. You can deal with the problem better if you try to understand the reason for your co-worker's attitude. Sometimes it's hard for individual employees to see themselves as part of the whole company. They each see only their small part. So they see any work that isn't "theirs" as extra. Try to help your co-worker understand this: In successful companies, the employees all work together to help the company reach its goals. And when that happens, everybody benefits in many ways. Individual jobs become more meaningful. And the company's success could result in raises and promotions for employees. So working together as a team is really everybody's job, and it's in everyone's interest to see it that way.

Good luck!

3. Answer the QUESTIONS FOR PAIR A together.

QUESTIONS FOR PAIR A

   a. What is Annoyed's problem?

   _____

   b. What is one possible reason for the co-worker's attitude?

   _____

   c. What does Dr. Hartley advise Annoyed to do about the situation?

   _____

4. Find a Pair B with page 75. Answer their questions about your article.

5. Ask them the QUESTIONS TO ASK PAIR B. Write their answers.

QUESTIONS TO ASK PAIR B

   a. What is Frustrated's problem?

   _____

   b. What is a "control freak"?

   _____

   c. What does Dr. Hartley advise Frustrated to do about the situation?

   _____

KEEP GOING!

Talk about dealing with difficult people. Do you think it's possible to change another person's behavior by changing your own behavior? Why or why not?

Pair B: Dealing with Difficult Co-workers

1. Find a partner with page 75. You are Pair B.

2. Read the article.

Dr. Harry Hartley writes a popular advice column in the *Miami Star* about dealing with problems at work. Here is a letter he received from one reader last week, along with his advice.

Dear Dr. Hartley,

I'm having a big problem with a co-worker. Every time I start to do a job, he says, "Let *me* do it." I want to do my work, and I need to learn new skills, but my co-worker is preventing me from doing this. What should I do?

    Frustrated

Dear Frustrated,

It sounds like your co-worker is a "control freak"— a person who feels a need to be responsible for everything. A control freak sends the message, "Nobody can do the job better than I can." If you try to understand this behavior, you can probably improve the situation. Control freaks usually don't feel as confident as they seem. In fact, they often worry that they won't succeed.

Try to help your co-worker feel more confident. Start by telling him that he does something really well. Then, ask for his advice. You can ask, "What's the best way to do this?" or "Am I doing this right?" If you show your co-worker that his advice is important to you, he may feel more comfortable about sharing responsibilities with you.

Good luck!

3. Answer the QUESTIONS FOR PAIR B together.

QUESTIONS FOR PAIR B

    a. What is Frustrated's problem?

    _____

    b. What is a "control freak"?

    _____

    c. What does Dr. Hartley advise Frustrated to do about the situation?

    _____

4. Find a Pair A with page 74. Ask them the QUESTIONS TO ASK PAIR A. Write their answers.

QUESTIONS TO ASK PAIR A

    a. What is Annoyed's problem?

    _____

    b. What is one possible reason for the co-worker's attitude?

    _____

    c. What does Dr. Hartley advise Annoyed to do about the situation?

    _____

5. Answer Pair A's questions about your article.

KEEP GOING!

Talk about dealing with difficult people. Do you think it's possible to change another person's behavior by changing your own behavior?

Know What to Do and Say

The Project: Create a Do/Say chart for interpersonal skills
Supplies: chart paper, markers
Resources: dictionaries

When you respond to feedback, you...	
Do this:	Say this:
Listen.	OK.
Ask for clarification.	Do you mean...
Express thanks.	Thanks. I'll work on it.

1. Work with 3–5 students. Introduce yourself.

2. Choose your job.

   Leader: Help your team work together and watch the time.
   Recorder: Write the team's ideas.
   Supplier: Get the supplies and the resources.
   Researcher: Find information to help your team complete the project.
   Reporter: Tell the class about the project.

3. Choose a skill for your Do/Say chart: make suggestions, manage conflict, work on a team, respond to feedback, or another skill of your choice.

4. Brainstorm some things you do and say for your skill.

   Leader: Give the team 10 minutes. Ask each person for ideas.
   Recorder: Write the name and ideas of each team member.

5. Create the Do/Say chart.

   Supplier: Get the supplies and the resources from your teacher.
   Recorder:
   • Write *When you_____ , you* . . . at the top of the chart. Complete the heading with your skill.
   • Make two columns under the heading. Label the columns *Do this:* and *Say this:*.
   Team: List the things you do and say. Write as many as you can.
   Researcher: Use a dictionary to help your team with vocabulary and spelling.

6. Show your project to the class.

   Reporter: Show the class your team's chart. Point out the two best ideas of things to do and say.

KEEP GOING!
Exchange charts with another team. Add at least two more ideas to the other team's chart.

Unit 7 Buy Now, Pay Later

Lesson 1: Picture Differences
All About Finances
Picture A 78
Picture B 79

Lesson 2: Round Table Writing 80
Can You Put a Price on Happiness?

Lesson 3
Peer Dictation: Time and Money 81
Survey: If You Won $1,000,000 82

Lesson 4: Role-Play 83
Let's Make It $150 a Month

Lesson 5: Jigsaw Reading
Super Savers
Pair A 84
Pair B 85

Review and Expand
Team Project: A Budget for Our Party 86

Picture A: All About Finances

1. Find a partner with Picture B (page 79). Don't show this paper to your partner!

2. Work with your partner to find 10 differences between your pictures.

3. Write the picture differences in the chart below

	Picture A	**Picture B**
1.	*The interest rate for a home loan is 6.99%.*	*The interest rate for a home loan is 5.99%.*
2.		
3.		
4.		
5.		
6.		
7.		
8.		
9.		
10.		

KEEP GOING!
Talk about loans. What are some things that people borrow money to pay for?

Picture B: All About Finances

1. Find a partner with Picture A (page 78). Don't show this paper to your partner!

2. Work with your partner to find 10 differences between your pictures.

3. Write the picture differences in the chart below.

	Picture A	Picture B
1.	*The interest rate for a home loan is 6.99%.*	*The interest rate for a home loan is 5.99%.*
2.		
3.		
4.		
5.		
6.		
7.		
8.		
9.		
10.		

KEEP GOING!
Talk about loans. What are some things that people borrow money to pay for?

Can You Put a Price on Happiness?

1. Work with 3 classmates.
2. Look at the picture. Read the first sentence.
3. Brainstorm sentences about the pictures.
4. Take turns writing sentences to continue the story.
5. Check your spelling in a dictionary.

Who seems happier, Rich or Harry?

_____

_____

_____

_____

_____

_____

_____

_____

KEEP GOING!

Exchange stories with another group. What do you find interesting, surprising, or funny about their story?

Time and Money

Partner A
• **Read a sentence to Partner B.** • **Listen to Partner B repeat the sentence.**   **Is it correct? If not, say it again.**
1. Aldo wouldn't have to pay late fees if he paid his bills on time. 2. If he didn't have to pay late fees, he'd have more money. 3. If he had more money, he would pay his credit card balances faster. 4. If he paid his balances faster, he wouldn't have any debts.
• **Listen to Partner B say a sentence.** • **Repeat the sentence.** • **Write the sentence.**
5.
6.
7.
8.

- -Fold Here- -

Partner B
• **Listen to Partner A say a sentence.** • **Repeat the sentence.** • **Write the sentence.**
1.
2.
3.
4.
• **Read a sentence to Partner A.** • **Listen to Partner A repeat the sentence.**   **Is it correct? If not, say it again.**
5. Rico would have more time if he didn't watch so much TV. 6. If Rico had more time, he would look for a better job. 7. If he got a better job, he would have more money. 8. If he didn't watch so much TV, he would have more money.

KEEP GOING!

Write 5 sentences about what you would do if you had a lot of free time.

Talk about your sentences with a partner.

If I had six months of free time, I would travel around the world.

If You Won $1,000,000

1. Read the questions. Write your answers in the chart.
2. Ask your classmates the questions in the chart.
3. Write your classmates' names and answers in the chart.
4. Use complete sentences to answer your classmates' questions.

If you won $1,000,000, would you . . .	My answers	_____'s answers	_____'s answers	_____'s answers
buy a house?				
quit your job?				
travel around the world?				
use some of the money to help other people?				
give money to your family and friends?				
continue to study English?				

5. Work with a partner. Compare your charts. Write 6 sentences.

Marco and Laura would buy a house, but Martin wouldn't.

1. _____
2. _____
3. _____
4. _____
5. _____
6. _____

KEEP GOING!

If you won a lot of money, would you make big changes in your life? Why or why not? Talk about your opinions with the class.

Let's Make It $150 a Month

1. Work with 3 classmates. Say all the lines in the script.
2. Choose your character.
3. Finish the conversation. Write more lines for each character.
4. Practice the lines.
5. Act out the role-play with your group.

Scene	**Characters**	**Props**
At the kitchen table	• Parent 1 • Child 1 • Parent 2 • Child 2	• A pad of paper • A pen or pencil

The Script

Parent 1: If we want to take a vacation next summer, we should start saving now.

Child 1: How much do we need to save?

Parent 2: We should save at least $150 a month.

Child 2: That's a lot of money! How are we going to do it?.

Parent 1: How about if I start giving everyone haircuts at home?

Parent 2: If I were you, I'd think of something else. You don't know how to cut hair.

Parent 1: Well, maybe not. What if we had "movie night" at home instead of going out?

Child 1: You mean rent movies and make our own popcorn and snacks?

Parent 2: Yes. That saves us $100 right there. What else can we do?

KEEP GOING!

Watch your classmates' role-plays. Write the answers to these questions: How do the children decide to save money? How much will the family save every month?

Pair A: Super Savers

1. Find a partner with page 84. You are Pair A.

2. Read the article.

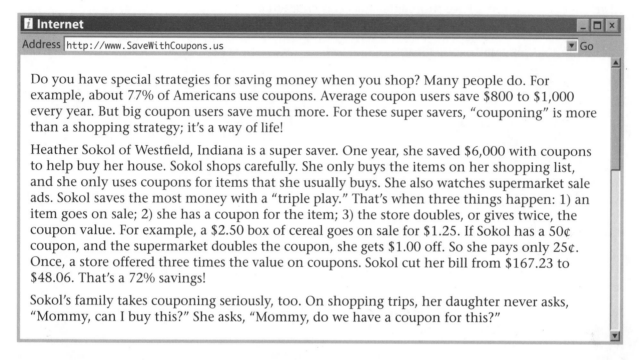

Internet

Address http://www.SaveWithCoupons.us ▼ Go

Do you have special strategies for saving money when you shop? Many people do. For example, about 77% of Americans use coupons. Average coupon users save $800 to $1,000 every year. But big coupon users save much more. For these super savers, "couponing" is more than a shopping strategy; it's a way of life!

Heather Sokol of Westfield, Indiana is a super saver. One year, she saved $6,000 with coupons to help buy her house. Sokol shops carefully. She only buys the items on her shopping list, and she only uses coupons for items that she usually buys. She also watches supermarket sale ads. Sokol saves the most money with a "triple play." That's when three things happen: 1) an item goes on sale; 2) she has a coupon for the item; 3) the store doubles, or gives twice, the coupon value. For example, a $2.50 box of cereal goes on sale for $1.25. If Sokol has a 50¢ coupon, and the supermarket doubles the coupon, she gets $1.00 off. So she pays only 25¢. Once, a store offered three times the value on coupons. Sokol cut her bill from $167.23 to $48.06. That's a 72% savings!

Sokol's family takes couponing seriously, too. On shopping trips, her daughter never asks, "Mommy, can I buy this?" She asks, "Mommy, do we have a coupon for this?"

3. Answer the QUESTIONS FOR PAIR A together.

QUESTIONS FOR PAIR A

   a. What are two ways Heather Sokol shops carefully?

   _____

   b. When does Sokol save the most money?

   _____

   c. How do you know that Sokol's family takes couponing seriously?

   _____

4. Find a Pair B with page 85. Answer their questions about your article.

5. Ask them the QUESTIONS TO ASK PAIR B. Write their answers.

QUESTIONS TO ASK PAIR B

   a. What are two ways Kim Gilmore gets coupons?

   _____

   b. How does Gilmore get her biggest savings?

   _____

   c. Why don't Gilmore and her mother agree about price-matching?

   _____

KEEP GOING!

Talk about shopping strategies. What are some other ways to save money when you shop?

Pair B: Super Savers

1. Find a partner with page 85. You are Pair B.

2. Read the article.

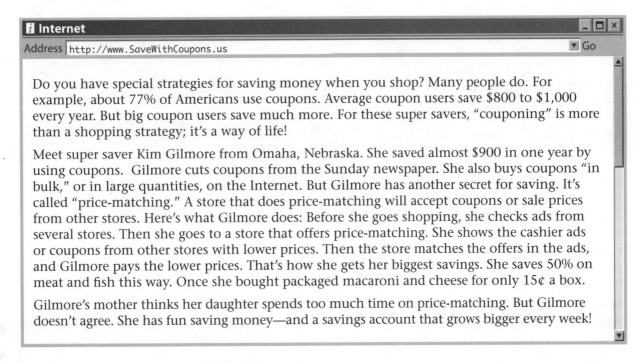

i Internet

Address http://www.SaveWithCoupons.us   ▼ Go

Do you have special strategies for saving money when you shop? Many people do. For example, about 77% of Americans use coupons. Average coupon users save $800 to $1,000 every year. But big coupon users save much more. For these super savers, "couponing" is more than a shopping strategy; it's a way of life!

Meet super saver Kim Gilmore from Omaha, Nebraska. She saved almost $900 in one year by using coupons. Gilmore cuts coupons from the Sunday newspaper. She also buys coupons "in bulk," or in large quantities, on the Internet. But Gilmore has another secret for saving. It's called "price-matching." A store that does price-matching will accept coupons or sale prices from other stores. Here's what Gilmore does: Before she goes shopping, she checks ads from several stores. Then she goes to a store that offers price-matching. She shows the cashier ads or coupons from other stores with lower prices. Then the store matches the offers in the ads, and Gilmore pays the lower prices. That's how she gets her biggest savings. She saves 50% on meat and fish this way. Once she bought packaged macaroni and cheese for only 15¢ a box.

Gilmore's mother thinks her daughter spends too much time on price-matching. But Gilmore doesn't agree. She has fun saving money—and a savings account that grows bigger every week!

3. Answer the QUESTIONS FOR PAIR B together.

QUESTIONS FOR PAIR B

    a. What are two ways Kim Gilmore gets coupons?

    _____

    b. How does Gilmore get her biggest savings?

    _____

    c. Why don't Gilmore and her mother agree about price-matching?

    _____

4. Find a Pair A with page 84. Ask them the QUESTIONS TO ASK PAIR A. Write their answers.

QUESTIONS TO ASK PAIR A

    a. What are two ways Heather Sokol shops carefully?

    _____

    b. When does Sokol save the most money?

    _____

    c. How do you know that Sokol's family takes couponing seriously?

    _____

5. Answer Pair A's questions about your article.

KEEP GOING!

Talk about shopping strategies. What are some other ways to save money when you shop?

A Budget for Our Party

The Project: Make a budget for a class party
Supplies: notebook paper, pens, or a word processing program (if computers are available)
Resources: dictionaries, supermarket ads, a calculator (optional)

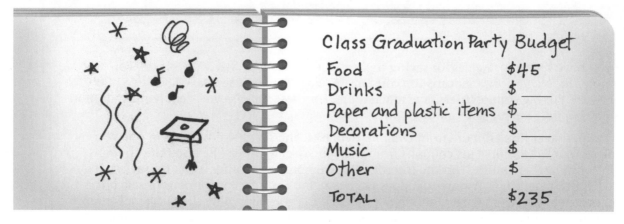

Class Graduation Party Budget
Food $45
Drinks $ ____
Paper and plastic items $ ____
Decorations $ ____
Music $ ____
Other $ ____
TOTAL $235

1. Work with 3–5 students. Introduce yourself.

2. Choose your job.

   Leader: Help your team work together and watch the time.
   Recorder: Write the team's ideas.
   Supplier: Get the supplies and the resources.
   Researcher: Find information to help your team complete the project.
   Reporter: Tell the class about the project.

3. Imagine that you have $250 to spend on a class party. Decide what kind of party you want to have. Then brainstorm items you will need in these categories: food, drinks, paper and plastic items, decorations, music, and miscellaneous.

   Leader: Give the team 5 minutes.
   Recorder: Write the name and ideas of each team member.

4. Make the budget.

   Supplier: Get the supplies and the resources from your teacher.
   Team:
   • Use supermarket ads to help you find the items you need and their prices.
   • Organize the items into categories. Write the categories on your budget.
   • Add up the costs for each category. Write the amounts on your budget.
   • Add up all the costs to figure out your total budget. Make sure the total is $250 or less.
   Researcher: Use a dictionary to help the team with vocabulary and spelling.

5. Show your project to the class.

   Reporter: Tell the class about your team's budget decisions. Which items will cost the most? Which ones will cost the least?

KEEP GOING!
Compare all the teams' budgets. Decide which plan is the best one. Explain why.

Unit 8 Satisfaction Guaranteed

Lesson 1: Picture Differences
Where Will She Find a Gift?
Picture A 88
Picture B 89

Lesson 2: Round Table Writing 90
What a Disappointment!

Lesson 3
Peer Dictation: Not What They Expected 91
Survey: How Do You Feel about Shopping? 92

Lesson 4: Role-Play 93
I'd Like to Place an Order

Lesson 5: Jigsaw Reading
Ask Mike Mechanic
Pair A 94
Pair B 95

Review and Expand
Team Project: Consumer's Choice 96

Picture A: Where Will She Find a Gift?

1. Find a partner with Picture B (page 89). Don't show this paper to your partner!

2. Work with your partner to find 10 differences between your pictures.

3. Write the picture differences in the chart below.

	Picture A	**Picture B**
1.	The online store is E-buy.us.	The online store is Congo.us.
2.		
3.		
4.		
5.		
6.		
7.		
8.		
9.		
10.		

KEEP GOING!

Is the way you shop today different from the way you shopped ten years ago? Explain.

Picture B: Where Will She Find a Gift?

1. Find a partner with Picture A (page 88). Don't show this paper to your partner!

2. Work with your partner to find 10 differences between your pictures.

3. Write the picture differences in the chart below.

	Picture A	**Picture B**
1.	*The online store is E-buy.us.*	*The online store is Congo.us.*
2.		
3.		
4.		
5.		
6.		
7.		
8.		
9.		
10.		

KEEP GOING!

Is the way you shop today different from the way you shopped ten years ago? Explain.

What a Disappointment!

1. Work with 3 classmates.

2. Look at the picture. Read the first sentence.

3. Brainstorm sentences about the pictures.

4. Take turns writing sentences to continue the story.

5. Check your spelling in a dictionary.

Magda wanted a new toaster.

KEEP GOING!

Exchange stories with another group. What do you find interesting, surprising, or funny about their story?

Not What They Expected

Partner A
• **Read a sentence to Partner B.** • **Listen to Partner B repeat the sentence.**   **Is it correct? If not, say it again.**
1. Salina was pretty excited when her new coffee maker arrived. 2. Unfortunately, the owner's manual was very confusing. 3. The coffee pot was scratched, and the plug was defective, too. 4. I wasn't surprised when she returned it.
• **Listen to Partner B say a sentence.** • **Repeat the sentence.** • **Write the sentence.**
5.
6.
7.
8.

- FOLD HERE -

Partner B
• **Listen to Partner A say a sentence.** • **Repeat the sentence.** • **Write the sentence.**
1.
2.
3.
4.
• **Read a sentence to Partner A.** • **Listen to Partner A repeat the sentence.**   **Is it correct? If not, say it again.**
5. Bill was very disappointed with the jeans he bought online. 6. He was pretty excited when they came in the mail. 7. Unfortunately, the jeans were torn and dirty. 8. It was an extremely disappointing experience.

KEEP GOING!

Write 5 sentences about movies, sports events, or TV shows you have seen.
Talk about the sentences with your partner.
River Dogs *was supposed to be a really interesting movie, but I was bored.*

How Do You Feel about Shopping?

1. Read the questions. Write your answers in the chart.

2. Ask your classmates the questions in the chart.

3. Write your classmates' names and answers in the chart.

4. Use complete sentences to answer your classmates' questions.

Ask and answer these questions.	My answers	_____'s answers	_____'s answers	_____'s answers
Do you think shopping is interesting or boring?				
Have you ever been disappointed with something you ordered from a catalog?				
Which is more exciting to you, a shopping network or a flea market?				
Were you ever surprised by a shopping experience?				
Is it easy or confusing to buy things online?				

5. Work with a partner. Compare your charts. Write 6 sentences.

Joy and I think shopping is interesting, but Ed thinks it's boring.

1. _____

2. _____

3. _____

4. _____

5. _____

6. _____

KEEP GOING!

What is the most interesting shopping experience you've ever had?
Talk about your experience with the class.

I'd Like to Place an Order

1. Work with 2 classmates. Say all the lines in the script.
2. Choose your character.
3. Finish the conversation. Write more lines for each character.
4. Practice the lines.
5. Act out the role-play with your group.

Scene	**Characters**	**Props**
On the phone	• Salesperson • Customer • Sales Manager	Two telephones

The Script

Salesperson: Thank you for calling Kitchen Tools. How may I help you?

Customer: I'd like to place an order from your catalog.

Salesperson: Sure. Could you please give me the item number?

Customer: Yes. It's BP2000.

Salesperson: The electric banana peeler. I'll see if it's available. Could you please hold?

Customer: Yes, of course.

Salesperson: Do we still have item number BP2000?

Sales Manager: I'm afraid not. Those banana peelers were so popular that they're all sold out.

Salesperson: What should I say to the customer?

KEEP GOING!

Watch your classmates' role-plays. Write the answers to these questions: What does the salesperson say to the customer? What does the customer respond?

Pair A: Ask Mike Mechanic

1. Find a partner with page 94. You are Pair A.

2. Read the article.

Question: When is a car not a car?

Answer: When it's a lemon!

Does that answer surprise you? In fact, *lemon* is the common name for a car with many problems. New cars are usually problem-free. There are 17 million new cars sold each year in the U.S., and only 1% of them have problems. But when they do, the owners can write to Mike Mechanic for advice. Mike answers these letters on his website.

Dear Mike,

I'm writing to you because my new car has had nothing but problems since the day I bought it. The first time I turned on the headlights, the windshield wipers went on, and they didn't stop until I turned off the ignition. Then every time I turned on the radio, the trunk popped open! The mechanic at the car dealer tried to fix the problems, but he didn't succeed. It's impossible to drive the car like this!

And now I have another problem. When I try to open the windows, they start to go up and down all by themselves. In fact, I think they're still going! I have to take the car back to the dealer again. My friend says the car is a lemon, and that there are special laws to protect consumers like me. Can you tell me more about this?

Disappointed

3. Answer the QUESTIONS FOR PAIR A together.

QUESTIONS FOR PAIR A

a. Why is the car owner writing to Mike Mechanic?

_____

b. What are two problems with the car?

_____

c. What does the car owner want to find out from Mike?

_____

4. Find a Pair B with page 95. Answer their questions about your article.

5. Ask them the QUESTIONS TO ASK PAIR B. Write their answers.

QUESTIONS TO ASK PAIR B

a. What kind of cars do lemon laws apply to?

_____

b. If you think your car is a lemon, what are two questions to ask yourself?

_____

c. What is Mike's suggestion for the car owner?

_____

KEEP GOING!

Talk about problems with big-ticket items. If you had problems with a new car, refrigerator, or other large purchase, what would you do?

Pair B: Ask Mike Mechanic

1. Find a partner with page 95. You are Pair B.

2. Read the article.

Question: When is a car not a car?

Answer: When it's a lemon!

Does that answer surprise you? In fact, *lemon* is the common name for cars with problems that can't be fixed. New cars are usually problem free. There are 17 million new cars sold each year in the U.S., and only 1% of them have problems. But when they do, the owners can write to Mike Mechanic for advice. Mike answers these letters on his website.

Dear Disappointed,

You sure do have a lot of problems with your new car. The good news is that every state has a lemon law, which applies to new cars and cars under warranty. Let's figure out if your car really is a lemon.

1. Did you have the problems before you'd driven 12,000 miles or before the car was one year old?

2. Has the problem continued after three or four visits to the dealer? Or, has the car been in the repair shop for a total of 30 days? If you answered "yes" to both questions, your car is probably a lemon.

I suggest that you contact an attorney who specializes in the lemon law in your state. You may have the right to receive a refund or a replacement car. I hope you can turn your sour experience into a sweeter one soon!

Mike

3. Answer the QUESTIONS FOR PAIR B together.

QUESTIONS FOR PAIR B

    a. What kind of cars do lemon laws apply to?

    _____

    b. If you think your car is a lemon, what are two questions to ask yourself?

    _____

    c. What is Mike's suggestion for the car owner?

    _____

4. Find a Pair A with page 94. Ask them the QUESTIONS TO ASK PAIR A. Write their answers.

QUESTIONS TO ASK PAIR A

    a. Why is the car owner writing to Mike Mechanic?

    _____

    b. What are two problems with the car?

    _____

    c. What does the car owner want to find out from Mike?

    _____

5. Answer Pair A's questions about your article.

KEEP GOING!

Talk about problems with big-ticket items. If you had problems with a new car, refrigerator, or other large purchase, what would you do?

Consumer's Choice

The Project: Make a consumer satisfaction chart and rate a product
Supplies: chart paper, markers, scissors, glue
Resources: dictionaries, magazines

Cell Phone XZ2000

	Extremely Satisfied	Very Satisfied	Somewhat Satisfied	Not Satisfied
Quality			✓	
Sound		✓		
Easy to use				✓

1. Work with 3–5 students. Introduce yourself.

2. Choose your job.

> **Leader:** Help your team work together and watch the time.
> **Recorder:** Write the team's ideas.
> **Supplier:** Get the supplies and the resources.
> **Researcher:** Find more information to help your team complete the project.
> **Reporter:** Tell the class about the project.

3. As a team, chose a product to rate: a microwave oven, a computer, a cell phone, a car, or another product of your choice.

4. Brainstorm the categories you need to rate your product.

> **Leader:** Give the team 5 minutes. Ask each person for ideas.
> **Recorder:** Write the name and ideas of each team member.

5. Make the rating chart.

> **Supplier:** Get the supplies and the resources from your teacher.
> **Team:**
> • Write the name of the product at the top of the paper.
> • Make the chart: List the categories of satisfaction across the top. List the rating categories down the left side.
> • Draw or find a picture of the product to add to your chart.
> • Use your chart to rate your product. Use checkmarks to show your satisfaction in each category.
> • Decide on a general rating for your product.

6. Show your project to the class.

> **Reporter:** Tell the class what general rating your team gave your product. Explain why.

KEEP GOING!
Exchange charts with another team. Use their chart to rate another product.

Unit 9 Take Care!

Lesson 1: Picture Differences
Take Good Care of Yourself
Picture A 98
Picture B 99

Lesson 2: Round Table Writing 100
Getting Started Was the Hardest Part

Lesson 3
Peer Dictation: A Lot of Advice 101
Survey: What You Should Do.. 102

Lesson 4: Role-Play.. 103
Is There Anything Else You'd Recommend?

Lesson 5: Jigsaw Reading
What's a Centenarian?
Pair A 104
Pair B 105

Review and Expand
Team Project: An Ounce of Prevention 106

Picture A: Take Good Care of Yourself

1. Find a partner with Picture B (page 99). Don't show this paper to your partner!

2. Work with your partner to find 10 differences between your pictures.

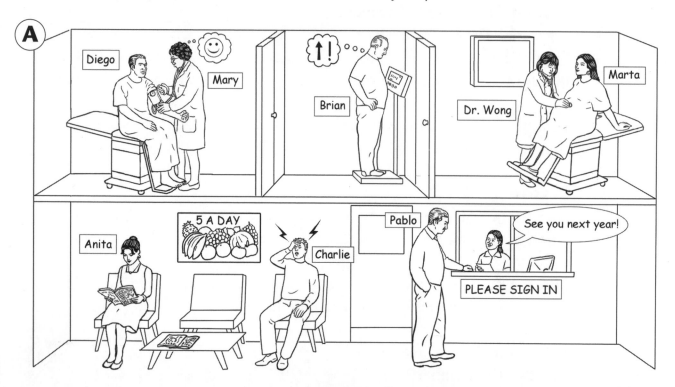

3. Write the picture differences in the chart below.

	Picture A	Picture B
1.	Pablo will return for his yearly physical.	Pablo will return for a medical screening.
2.		
3.		
4.		
5.		
6.		
7.		
8.		
9.		
10.		

KEEP GOING!

Talk about staying healthy. What are the three most important things you can do to prevent health problems?

Picture B: Take Good Care of Yourself

1. Find a partner with Picture A (page 98). Don't show this paper to your partner!

2. Work with your partner to find 10 differences between your pictures.

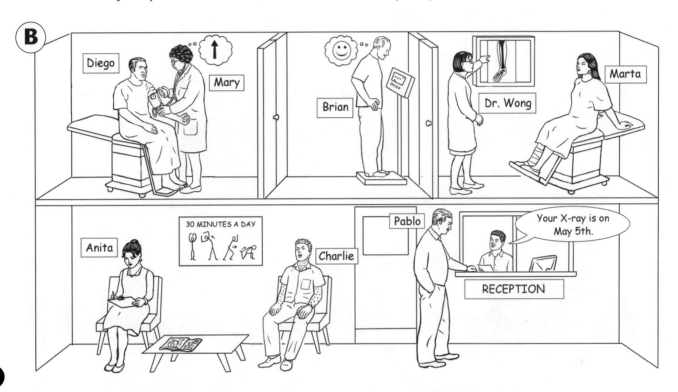

3. Write the picture differences in the chart below.

	Picture A	**Picture B**
1.	*Pablo will return for his yearly physical.*	*Pablo will return for a medical screening.*
2.		
3.		
4.		
5.		
6.		
7.		
8.		
9.		
10.		

KEEP GOING!

Talk about staying healthy. What are the three most important things you can do to prevent health problems?

Getting Started Was the Hardest Part

1. Work with 3 classmates.
2. Look at the picture. Read the first sentence.
3. Brainstorm sentences about the pictures.
4. Take turns writing sentences to continue the story.
5. Check your spelling in a dictionary.

Before   After

It was hard for Jerry to start a daily exercise program, but now he's really glad he did.

_____

_____

_____

_____

_____

_____

_____

KEEP GOING!

Exchange stories with another group. What do you find interesting, surprising, or funny about their story?

A Lot of Advice

Partner A
• **Read a sentence to Partner B.** • **Listen to Partner B repeat the sentence.**   **Is it correct? If not, say it again.**
1. Joe and Max should take better care of their health. 2. Joe shouldn't forget to drink more water every day. 3. Max ought to eat more fruits and vegetables. 4. They'd better get yearly physicals, too.
• **Listen to Partner B say a sentence.** • **Repeat the sentence.** • **Write the sentence.**
5.
6.
7.
8.

- FOLD HERE -

Partner B
• **Listen to Partner A say a sentence.** • **Repeat the sentence.** • **Write the sentence.**
1.
2.
3.
4.
• **Read a sentence to Partner A.** • **Listen to Partner A repeat the sentence.**   **Is it correct? If not, say it again.**
5. You and I shouldn't work as hard as we do. 6. I should find a job with shorter hours. 7. You'd better not work seven days a week anymore. 8. We've got to have more time to relax.

> **KEEP GOING!**
> Write 5 questions about health advice. Read the questions to your partner. Ask your partner to answer the questions.
> *How often should people exercise? / I think people should exercise every day.*

What You Should Do

1. Read the questions. Write your answers in the chart.
2. Ask your classmates the questions in the chart.
3. Write your classmates' names and answers in the chart.
4. Use complete sentences to answer your classmates' questions.

Ask and answer these questions.	My answers	_____'s answers	_____'s answers	_____'s answers
What is one thing you should do if you want to lose weight?				
What is something you ought to do every day if you want to feel great?				
What is something you'd better not do if you want to stay healthy?				
What is one thing you shouldn't do if you're sick?				
What is one thing you should remember when you take medicine?				

5. Work with a partner. Compare your charts. Write 6 sentences.

   Lucia says you should exercise if you want to lose weight.

1. _____
2. _____
3. _____
4. _____
5. _____
6. _____

KEEP GOING!

Is it easy or difficult to stay healthy? Talk about your opinions with the class.

Is There Anything Else You'd Recommend?

1. Work with 2 classmates. Say all the lines in the script.
2. Choose your character.
3. Finish the conversation. Write more lines for each character.
4. Practice the lines.
5. Act out the role-play with your group.

Scene

A doctor's office

Characters

- Doctor
- Patient
- Nurse

Props

- A folder
- A piece of paper
- A pen

The Script

Doctor: Do you have any more questions?

Patient: Yes, doctor. How's my blood pressure?

Doctor: Could you bring me the patient's folder?

Nurse: I've got it right here. Your blood pressure has gone down a lot.

Doctor: That's excellent. Have you made any changes in your habits?

Patient: Well, I've cut back on salt recently.

Nurse: Cutting back on salt is a good start.

Doctor: You should also consider exercising.

Patient: So I should continue watching my diet and start to exercise. Is there anything else you'd recommend?

KEEP GOING!

Watch your classmates' role-plays. Write the answers to these questions: What else do the doctor and the nurse recommend? What does the patient say?

Pair A: What's a Centenarian?

1. Find a partner with page 104. You are Pair A.

2. Read the article.

What's a centenarian? It's the name for a person who is 100 years old or older. In the world today, there are about 80,000 centenarians. What helps centenarians live so long? Is it the place they live? Or are there other more important reasons? Scientists often look at the lives of individuals to answer these questions.

Antonio Todde was a centenarian who lived to be 112. He was born in 1889 to a poor family in Sardinia, Italy. He spent most of his life taking care of sheep (a farm animal). That's why he did a lot of walking, sometimes for days at a time. Mr. Todde lived a simple life, and he ate only pasta[1], vegetable soup, meat, and cheese. His father lived to be 90,

his mother lived to be 99, and one sister lived to be 100.

Scientists have found that nearly twice as many people in Sardinia reach their 100th birthday as people who live in other places. But before you decide to move to Sardinia, you should know this: Scientists think that heredity and a healthy diet are also important reasons for the long lives of Sardinians. How does Mr. Todde explain his long life? On his 112th birthday, he told reporters his secret. He said, "Just love your brother," and "Take one day after the other."

[1]pasta: an Italian noodle made of flour and water, and cut into different shapes

3. Answer the QUESTIONS FOR PAIR A together.

QUESTIONS FOR PAIR A

   a. When and where was Antonio Todde born?

_____

   b. What did he do for most of his life?

_____

   c. What are two possible reasons for Mr. Todde's long life?

_____

4. Find a Pair B with page 105. Answer their questions about your article.

5. Ask them the QUESTIONS FOR PAIR B. Write their answers.

QUESTIONS TO ASK PAIR B

   a. When and where was Kamato Hongo born?

_____

   b. What kind of work did she do?

_____

   c. What are two possible reasons for Mrs. Hongo's long life?

_____

KEEP GOING!

Talk about long lives. In your opinion, what is the most important reason why some people live to a very old age?

Pair B: What's a Centenarian?

1. Find a partner with page 105. You are Pair B.

2. Read the article.

What's a centenarian? It's the name for a person who is 100 years old or older. In the world today, there are about 80,000 centenarians. What helps centenarians live so long? Is it the place they live? Or are there other more important reasons? Scientists often look at the lives of individuals to answer these questions.

Kamato Hongo was a centenarian who lived to be 116. She was born in 1887, on Tokunoshima Island in southern Japan. Japan is a country known for the long lives of its people.

Mrs. Hongo and her husband worked as farmers for most of their lives. Her diet included fish, rice, pork[1], and green tea, with occasional sweet treats made from brown

sugar. What was Mrs. Hongo's secret? Was her diet the reason she lived so long? Her daughter said that Mrs. Hongo preferred natural food. Mrs. Hongo also exercised regularly. Even after she had to stay in bed after an illness, she exercised to music, using her arms to perform *Teodori*, a traditional dance of her island. Mrs. Hongo always lived in a loving environment with her family around her. Some people think that was the reason she lived to be 116. How did Mrs. Hongo explain her long life? She often talked about the importance of a positive attitude. Her simple recipe: "Don't worry too much."

[1]pork: a type of meat that comes from a pig

3. Answer the QUESTIONS FOR PAIR B together.

QUESTIONS FOR PAIR B

  a. When and where was Kamato Hongo born?

  _____

  b. What kind of work did she do?

  _____

  c. What are two possible reasons for Mrs. Hongo's long life?

  _____

4. Find a Pair A with page 104. Ask them the QUESTIONS FOR PAIR A. Write their answers.

QUESTIONS TO ASK PAIR A

  a. When and where was Antonio Todde born?

  _____

  b. What did he do for most of his life?

  _____

  c. What are two possible reasons for Mr. Todde's long life?

  _____

5. Answer Pair A's questions about your article.

KEEP GOING!

Talk about long lives. In your opinion, what is the most important reason why some people live to a very old age?

An Ounce of Prevention

The Project: Create a word web about staying healthy
Supplies: chart paper and markers
Resources: dictionaries, medical brochures, health websites

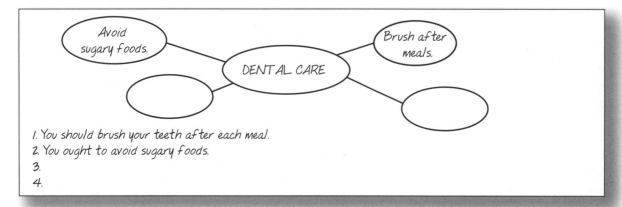

1. You should brush your teeth after each meal.
2. You ought to avoid sugary foods.
3.
4.

1. Work with 3–5 students. Introduce yourself.

2. Choose your job.

Leader: Help your team work together and watch the time.
Recorder: Write the team's ideas.
Supplier: Get the supplies and the resources.
Researcher: Find information to help your team complete the project.
Reporter: Tell the class about the project.

3. As a team, choose a topic for your word web: dental care, mental health, nutrition, prenatal care, or another topic of your choice.

4. Brainstorm some good health habits for your topic.

Leader: Give the team 5 minutes. Ask each person for ideas.
Recorder: Write the name and ideas of each team member.

5. Create the word web.

Supplier: Get the supplies and the resources from your teacher.
Team:
• Write your topic in the center of the paper and draw a circle around it.
• Write words or phrases for good health habits outside the circle. Draw a circle around each of these.
• Draw lines to connect the words and phrases to the topic.
• Write sentences under the word web, using the words and phrases in your web.
Researcher: Use a dictionary to help your team with vocabulary and spelling.

6. Show your project to the class.

Reporter: Tell the class about your team's word web. Ask them to add two more words or phrases to your web.

KEEP GOING!

Exchange word webs with another team. Write 2 more sentences about the other team's topic.

Unit 10 Get Involved!

Lesson 1: Picture Differences
Make It Happen!
Picture A 108
Picture B 109

Lesson 2: Round Table Writing 110
They're Very Concerned

Lesson 3
Peer Dictation: Do You Have Any Idea? 111
Survey: Do You Know Where the Courthouse Is? 112

Lesson 4: Role-Play 113
I Understand What You're Saying

Lesson 5: Jigsaw Reading
Volunteers Make a Difference
Pair A 114
Pair B 115

Review and Expand
Team Project: Make a Difference 116

Picture A: Make It Happen!

1. Find a partner with Picture B (page 109). Don't show this paper to your partner!

2. Work with your partner to find 10 differences between your pictures.

A

3. Write the picture differences in the chart below.

	Picture A	Picture B
1.	*Three people are identifying a problem in their community.*	*Two people are identifying a problem in their community.*
2.		
3.		
4.		
5.		
6.		
7.		
8.		
9.		
10.		

KEEP GOING!
Talk about problems in your community. What issues are the most important to you?

Picture B: Make It Happen!

1. Find a partner with Picture A (page 108). Don't show this paper to your partner!

2. Work with your partner to find 10 differences between your pictures.

3. Write the picture differences in the chart below.

	Picture A	**Picture B**
1.	*Three people are identifying a problem in their community.*	*Two people are identifying a problem in their community.*
2.		
3.		
4.		
5.		
6.		
7.		
8.		
9.		
10.		

> **KEEP GOING!**
> Talk about problems in your community. What issues are the most important to you?

They're Very Concerned

1. Work with 3 classmates.
2. Look at the picture. Read the first sentence.
3. Brainstorm sentences about the pictures.
4. Take turns writing sentences to continue the story.
5. Check your spelling in a dictionary.

The people of Sunnyvale have identified some serious problems in town.

_____

_____

_____

_____

_____

_____

_____

KEEP GOING!

Exchange stories with another group. What is interesting or surprising about their stories?

Do You Have Any Idea?

Partner A
• **Read a sentence to Partner B.** • **Listen to Partner B repeat the sentence.**   **Is it correct? If not, say it again.**
1. Do you know when the next city council meeting is? 2. Could you tell me where the meeting will be? 3. Do you have any idea what the council plans to discuss? 4. Do you know if you're going to attend?
• **Listen to Partner B say a sentence.** • **Repeat the sentence.** • **Write the sentence.**
5.
6.
7.
8.

- - - - - - - - - - - - - - - - - FOLD HERE -

Partner B
• **Listen to Partner A say a sentence.** • **Repeat the sentence.** • **Write the sentence.**
1.
2.
3.
4.
• **Read a sentence to Partner A.** • **Listen to Partner A repeat the sentence.**   **Is it correct? If not, say it again.**
5. Do you know what happened at the meeting last month? 6. Can you tell me what proposals were approved? 7. Do you know if the mayor will be at the meeting this time? 8. Can you tell me why he wasn't at the last meeting?

KEEP GOING!

Work with your partner. Write 5 questions about community events. Read your questions to your partner. Ask your partner to write the answers.
Do you know when the next local election will be? / Yes, I think it will be next month.

Unit 10 Peer Dictation   **111**

Do You Know Where the Courthouse Is?

1. Read the questions. Write your answers in the chart.
2. Ask your classmates the questions in the chart.
3. Write your classmates' names and answers in the chart.
4. Use complete sentences to answer your classmates' questions.

Do you know . . .	My answers	_____'s answers	_____'s answers	_____'s answers
where we can go to discuss community problems?				
where the courthouse is?				
when the next local election is?				
where we go to vote?				
where we can volunteer in our community?				

5. Work with a partner. Compare your charts. Write 6 sentences.

   Isabel says we can go to city council meetings to discuss community problems.

   1. _____
   2. _____
   3. _____
   4. _____
   5. _____
   6. _____

KEEP GOING!
What are some ways you can get more involved in your community? Talk about your opinions with the class.

I Understand What You're Saying

1. Work with 3 classmates. Say all the lines in the script.
2. Choose your character.
3. Finish the conversation. Write more lines for each character.
4. Practice the lines.
5. Act out the role-play with your group.

Scene

Town Hall

Characters

- Council Member 1
- Council Member 2
- Resident
- Council Member 3

Props

- A piece of paper
- A small hammer or gavel

The Script

Council Member 1: Quiet, everybody. I'd like to begin this public hearing on the summer rock concert.

Council Member 2: Please say your name and tell why you are here.

Resident: My name is Pat, and I live across from the park. I want to stop this concert.

Council Member 3: Could you tell us why?

Resident: There's already a lot of traffic and noise from the park. A concert will just make it worse.

Council Member 1: I understand what you're saying.

Council Member 2: Some people think that noise is music!

Council Member 3: Quiet, please. Let the resident speak.

Resident 1: Thank you. I think rock concerts are bad for the community.

Council Member 2: I'm not sure whether your neighbors agree with you. Do you think they do?

KEEP GOING!

Watch your classmates' role-plays. Write the answers to these questions: What does the resident say to Council Member 2? What do the council members decide?

Pair A: Volunteers Make a Difference

1. Find a partner with page 114. You are Pair A.
2. Read the article and letter.

Meals on Wheels Association of America (MOWAA) is an organization that provides meals to seniors and other people in need. It is the oldest and largest program of its kind in the U.S. MOWAA changes the lives of the one million people it serves. It can also make a big difference in the lives of its two million volunteers.

A volunteer from the Midwestern U.S. tells this story:

When my husband Ed and I retired, we started to volunteer for Meals on Wheels. We knew there were people who needed help, and we wanted to do something for our community. We delivered between 20 and 25 meals a day, five days a week, to people in a 170-mile area. Most of them didn't drive or have convenient public transportation. Getting meals from MOWAA allowed these people to stay in their homes and out of hospitals and retirement homes.

Ed and I saw that we were delivering more than hot meals. We were delivering a better way of life! That's something nobody can put a price on. Something else that's priceless is the feeling we got from our work. People often invited us into their homes and treated us like family. Volunteering for MOWAA is an experience we'll never forget.

Helen Carnino

3. Answer the QUESTIONS FOR PAIR A together.

QUESTIONS FOR PAIR A

a. What did Helen and Ed do as volunteers for the Meals on Wheels program?

_____

b. What did their help allow others to do?

_____

c. Why was their work with MOWAA an experience they will never forget?

_____

4. Find a Pair B with page 115. Answer their questions about your article.
5. Ask them the QUESTIONS FOR PAIR B. Write their answers.

QUESTIONS TO ASK PAIR B

a. Why did D.F. need the Meals on Wheels program?

_____

b. How did Helen and Ed help him?

_____

c. Why was D.F.'s experience with MOWAA something he will never forget?

_____

KEEP GOING!

Talk about volunteering. What kind of volunteer work would you like to do? Why?

Pair B: Volunteers Make a Difference

1. Find a partner with page 115. You are Pair B.

2. Read the article and letter.

Meals on Wheels Association of America (MOWAA) is an organization that provides meals to seniors and other people in need. It is the oldest and largest program of its kind in the U.S. MOWAA changes the lives of the one million people it serves. It can also make a big difference in the lives of its two million volunteers.

One person who received meals from MOWAA tells this story:

When I was 34 years old, I had a serious car accident. After ten days in the hospital, the doctors sent me home, but there was a problem. Because of my injuries, I couldn't drive to the store or prepare my own meals.

My family lived far away, and they couldn't take care of me. Then, someone at the hospital called Meals on Wheels. Soon, a wonderful couple began delivering hot meals to me, five days a week.

Having hot meals helped a lot, but meeting Helen and Ed was even more important. They cared about me, and their friendship helped me get better, physically and mentally. Because of them, I didn't have to stay in the hospital. I'm feeling great now, and I no longer need MOWAA. But I still talk with Helen and Ed on the phone. I'll never forget what they did for me.

D.F. George

3. Answer the QUESTIONS FOR PAIR B together.

QUESTIONS FOR PAIR B

    a. Why did D.F. need the Meals on Wheels program?

    _____

    b. How did Helen and Ed help him?

    _____

    c. Why was D.F.'s experience with MOWAA something he will never forget?

    _____

4. Find a Pair A with page 114. Ask them the QUESTIONS FOR PAIR A. Write their answers.

QUESTIONS TO ASK PAIR A

    a. What did Helen and Ed do as volunteers for the Meals on Wheels program?

    _____

    b. What did their help allow others to do?

    _____

    c. Why was their work with MOWAA an experience they will never forget?

    _____

5. Answer Pair A's questions about your article.

KEEP GOING!
Talk about volunteering. What kind of volunteer work would you like to do? Why?

Make a Difference

The Project: Create a poster about a community problem and solutions
Supplies: poster board, colored markers
Resources: dictionaries

	Problem: LITTER
	Solutions:
	• *Learn about recycling programs.*
	• *Start a neighborhood cleanup program.*
	•
	•
	Our plan for action: We will invite a speaker to talk to us about recycling.

1. Work with 3–5 students. Introduce yourself.

2. Choose your job.

> **Leader:** Help your team work together and watch the time.
> **Recorder:** Write the team's ideas.
> **Supplier:** Get the supplies and the resources.
> **Researcher:** Find more information to help your team complete the project.
> **Reporter:** Tell the class about the project.

3. As a team, choose one of the following community problems to solve: a dangerous intersection, homeless people, litter, graffiti, or another problem of your choice.

4. Brainstorm solutions for your problem.

> **Leader:** Give the team 5 minutes. Ask each person for ideas.
> **Recorder:** Write the name and ideas of each team member.

5. Make the poster.

> **Supplier:** Get the supplies and the resources from your teacher.
> **Team:**
> • Write the problem at the top of the poster.
> • List as many solutions as you can.
> • Decide on the action that your team will take and write it at the bottom.

6. Show your project to the class.

> **Reporter:** Describe your team's problem and your two best solutions.

KEEP GOING!
After all the teams have presented their posters, choose one problem and action plan.
Then, as a class, act on this plan to help solve the problem.

Unit 11　Find It On the Net

Lesson 1: Picture Differences
It's All on the Internet
Picture A 118
Picture B 119

Lesson 2: Round Table Writing 120
Some Things Will Never Change

Lesson 3
Peer Dictation: It Isn't Hard to Learn, Is It? 121
Survey: Using the Internet 122

Lesson 4: Role-Play 123
Can I Offer a Suggestion?

Lesson 5: Jigsaw Reading
Tenant-Landlord Problems
Pair A 124
Pair B 125

Review and Expand
Team Project: Welcome to Our Website! 126

Picture A: It's All on the Internet

1. Find a partner with Picture B (page 119). Don't show this paper to your partner!

2. Work with your partner to find 10 differences between your pictures.

3. Write the picture differences in the chart below.

	Picture A	**Picture B**
1.	*The pop-up ad is at the top of the page.*	*The pop-up ad is at the bottom of the page.*
2.		
3.		
4.		
5.		
6.		
7.		
8.		
9.		
10.		

KEEP GOING!

Talk about using websites. Do you like to search the Internet for information? Why or why not?

Picture B: It's All on the Internet

1. Find a partner with Picture A (page 118). Don't show this paper to your partner!

2. Work with your partner to find 10 differences between your pictures.

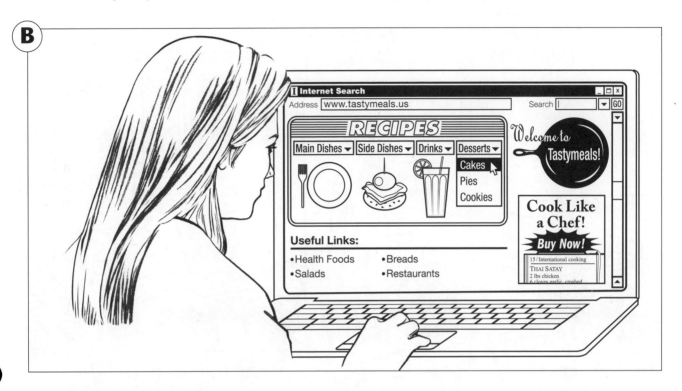

3. Write the picture differences in the chart below.

	Picture A	**Picture B**
1.	*The pop-up ad is at the top of the page.*	*The pop-up ad is at the bottom of the page.*
2.		
3.		
4.		
5.		
6.		
7.		
8.		
9.		
10.		

KEEP GOING!

Talk about using websites. Do you like to search the Internet for information?
Why or why not?

Some Things Will Never Change

1. Work with 3 classmates.

2. Look at the picture. Read the first sentence.

3. Brainstorm sentences about the pictures.

4. Take turns writing sentences to continue the story.

5. Check your spelling in a dictionary.

Technology has brought many changes to our daily lives, but some things will never change.

_____

_____

_____

_____

_____

_____

_____

_____

KEEP GOING!

Exchange stories with another group. What is interesting, surprising, or funny about their story?

It Isn't Hard to Learn, Is It?

Partner A
• **Read a sentence to Partner B.** • **Listen to Partner B repeat the sentence.**   **Is it correct? If not, say it again.**
1. Keeping in touch with friends is easy with email, isn't it? 2. You know how to send photos with email, don't you? 3. Everyone learns how to use email quickly, don't they? 4. It isn't hard to learn, is it?
• **Listen to Partner B say a sentence.** • **Repeat the sentence.** • **Write the sentence.**
5.
6.
7.
8.

- -Fold Here- -

Partner B
• **Listen to Partner A say a sentence.** • **Repeat the sentence.** • **Write the sentence.**
1.
2.
3.
4.
• **Read a sentence to Partner A.** • **Listen to Partner A repeat the sentence.**   **Is it correct? If not, say it again.**
5. The Internet is really great, isn't it? 6. Now you don't need to leave home to go shopping, do you? 7. Online stores offer all kinds of products, don't they? 8. But pop-up ads are annoying, aren't they?

KEEP GOING!

Work with your partner. Write 5 questions about technology.
It's quicker to write an email than a letter, isn't it?

Using the Internet

1. Read the questions. Write your answers in the chart.
2. Ask your classmates the questions in the chart.
3. Write your classmates' names and answers in the chart.
4. Use complete sentences to answer your classmates' questions.

Ask and answer these questions.	My answers	_____'s answers	_____'s answers	_____'s answers
You know how to use the Internet, don't you?				
You have some favorite websites, don't you?				
Getting the news online isn't difficult, is it?				
You don't shop online often, do you?				
Using the Internet is convenient, isn't it?				

5. Work with a partner. Compare your charts. Write 6 sentences.

   Most students know how to use the Internet.

   1. _____
   2. _____
   3. _____
   4. _____
   5. _____
   6. _____

KEEP GOING!
Think of one more question about the Internet. Ask your classmates the question.

Can I Offer a Suggestion?

1. Work with 2 classmates. Say all the lines in the script.
2. Choose your character.
3. Finish the conversation. Write more lines for each character.
4. Practice the lines.
5. Act out the role-play with your group.

Scene	Characters	Props
A coffee house	• Friend 1 • Friend 2 • Friend 3	Paper cups

The Script

Friend 1: Your landlord sent you your security deposit, didn't he?

Friend 2: No, he didn't. It's been almost three months since I moved out.

Friend 3: You already wrote him two letters, didn't you?

Friend 2: Yes, I did. But I still haven't received a response.

Friend 1: That's terrible! It's about time you got your refund.

Friend 3: It sure is. Can I offer a suggestion?

Friend 2: Please do. I'm ready to pull my hair out!

Friend 3: Why don't you send an email to the building manager?

Friend 1: That's a great idea! Why didn't I think of that?

Friend 2: What do you think I should say in the email?

KEEP GOING!

Watch your classmates' role-plays. Write the answers to these questions: What do the friends think Friend 2 should say in the email? Does Friend 2 decide to follow their advice?

Pair A: Tenant-Landlord Problems

1. Find a partner with page 124. You are Pair A.
2. Read the email.

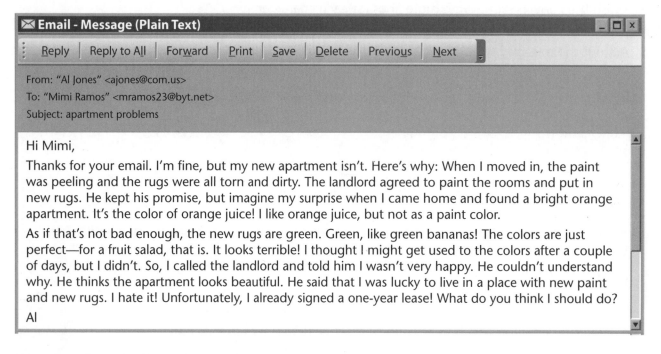

3. Answer the QUESTIONS FOR PAIR A together.

QUESTIONS FOR PAIR A

   a. What was wrong with the apartment before Al moved in?

   _____

   b. What changes did the landlord make?

   _____

   c. According to Al, how does the apartment look now?

   _____

4. Find a Pair B with page 125. Answer their questions about your email.
5. Ask them the QUESTIONS TO ASK PAIR B. Write their answers.

QUESTIONS TO ASK PAIR B

   a. What was the condition of the paint and the rugs when the tenant moved in?

   _____

   b. Why did Henry agree to change the paint and the rugs?

   _____

   c. According to Henry, how does the apartment look now?

   _____

KEEP GOING!

Talk about the emails. Who do you think is right, the tenant or the landlord?
What do you think each of them should do?

Pair B: Tenant-Landlord Problems

1. Find a partner with page 125. You are Pair B.

2. Read the email.

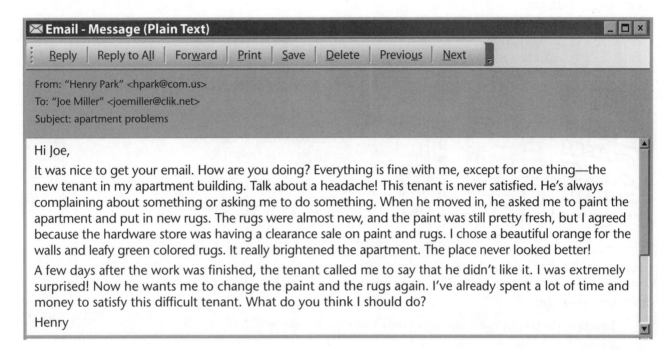

3. Answer the QUESTIONS FOR PAIR B together.

QUESTIONS FOR PAIR B

    a. What was the condition of the paint and the rugs when the tenant moved in?

    _____

    b. Why did Henry agree to change the paint and the rugs?

    _____

    c. According to Henry, how does the apartment look now?

    _____

4. Find a Pair A with page 124. Ask them the QUESTIONS TO ASK PAIR A. Write their answers.

QUESTIONS TO ASK PAIR A

    a. What was wrong with the apartment before Al moved in?

    _____

    b. What changes did the landlord make?

    _____

    c. According to Al, how does the apartment look now?

    _____

5. Answer Pair A's questions about your email.

> **KEEP GOING!**
>
> Talk about the emails. Who do you think is right, the tenant or the landlord?
> What do you think each of them should do?

Welcome to Our Website!

The Project: Create a web page for a class website
Supplies: chart paper or notebook paper, colored markers and pens, or a web-page composing program (if computers are available)
Resources: dictionaries, class calendars, brochures about the school

Little River Adult School

LITTLE RIVER ADULT SCHOOL

Our Class: Contact Information

Little River Adult School
English 401, Room 22
13261 Valley Boulevard
Norman, OK 73132

Phone: (405) 555-2000
Fax: (405) 555-2010

1. Work with 3–5 students. Introduce yourself.

2. Choose your job.

> **Leader:** Help your team work together and watch the time.
> **Recorder:** Write the team's ideas.
> **Supplier:** Get the supplies and the resources.
> **Researcher:** Find more information to help your team complete the project.
> **Graphic Designer:** Help your team design the web page.
> **Reporter:** Tell the class about the project.

3. As a team, choose a topic for your web page: class calendar, contact information, directions to our school, FAQs , study tips, or another topic of your choice.

4. Brainstorm ideas about the information you should include on your web page.

> **Leader:** Give the team 5 minutes. Ask each person for ideas.
> **Recorder:** Write the name and ideas of each team member.
> **Researcher:** Use the resources to find more information about your topic. Talk about the information with your team.

5. Design the web page.

> **Supplier:** Get the supplies and the resources from your teacher.
> **Team:**
> • Write as much information as you can about your topic.
> • Draw pictures or maps to make the information clearer and more interesting.
> **Graphic Designer:** Help your team organize the pictures and information.

6. Show your project to the class.

> **Reporter:** Tell the class about your web page

> **KEEP GOING!**
> Put all the teams' web pages together to create a class website.

Unit 12 How Did I Do?

Lesson 1: Picture Differences
Congratulations!
Picture A 128
Picture B 129

Lesson 2: Round Table Writing 130
Past Achievements, Future Goals

Lesson 3
Peer Dictation: Oscar Isn't Afraid of Working Hard 131
Survey: Do You Believe In Setting Goals? 132

Lesson 4: Role-Play 133
You're Doing a Great Job!

Lesson 5: Jigsaw Reading
Old Products, New Ideas
Pair A 134
Pair B 135

Review and Expand
Team Project: What's My Profession? 136

Picture A: Congratulations!

1. Find a partner with Picture B (page 129). Don't show this paper to your partner!

2. Work with your partner to find 10 differences between your pictures.

3. Write the picture differences in the chart below.

	Picture A	Picture B
1.	*Ana's dream is to open a clinic.*	*Ana's dream is to open a restaurant.*
2.		
3.		
4.		
5.		
6.		
7.		
8.		
9.		
10.		

KEEP GOING!
Talk about the future. What are some things you would like to achieve?

Picture B: Congratulations!

1. Find a partner with Picture A (page 128). Don't show this paper to your partner!

2. Work with your partner to find 10 differences between your pictures.

3. Write the picture differences in the chart below.

	Picture A	**Picture B**
1.	*Ana's dream is to open a clinic.*	*Ana's dream is to open a restaurant.*
2.		
3.		
4.		
5.		
6.		
7.		
8.		
9.		
10.		

KEEP GOING!

Talk about the future. What are some things you would like to achieve?

Past Achievements, Future Goals

1. Work with 3 classmates.

2. Look at the picture. Read the first sentence.

3. Brainstorm sentences about the picture.

4. Take turns writing sentences to continue the story.

5. Check your spelling in a dictionary.

Roberto is proud of his past achievements, and he's working on his goals for the future.

_____

_____

_____

_____

_____

_____

_____

_____

KEEP GOING!

Exchange stories with another group. What is interesting, surprising, or funny about their story?

Oscar Isn't Afraid of Working Hard

Partner A
• **Read a sentence to Partner B.** • **Listen to Partner B repeat the sentence. Is it correct? If not, say it again.**
1. Oscar isn't afraid of working hard. 2. He's really interested in getting ahead. 3. He's very excited about getting a promotion. 4. He looks forward to having more responsibility.
• **Listen to Partner B say a sentence.** • **Repeat the sentence.** • **Write the sentence!**
5.
6.
7.
8.

- - - - - - - - - - - - - - - - - - - -FOLD HERE- - - - - - - - - - - - - - - - - - - -

Partner B
• **Listen to Partner A say a sentence.** • **Repeat the sentence.** • **Write the sentence!**
1.
2.
3.
4.
• **Read a sentence to Partner A.** • **Listen to Partner A repeat the sentence. Is it correct? If not, say it again.**
5. Omar is very worried about changing jobs. 6. He isn't good at meeting new people. 7. He's also pretty nervous about using new technology. 8. He should really work on improving his skills.

KEEP GOING!

Work with your partner. Write 5 sentences to describe yourself or people you know.
My friend Sam is interested in learning Chinese.

Do You Believe In Setting Goals?

1. Read the questions. Write your answers in the chart.

2. Ask your classmates the questions in the chart.

3. Write your classmates' names and answers in the chart.

4. Use complete sentences to answer your classmates' questions.

Ask and answer these questions.	My answers	_____'s answers	_____'s answers	_____'s answers
What skills have you worked on improving in this class?				
Do you believe in setting goals?				
What kinds of courses are you interested in taking?				
What is one personal goal you look forward to achieving?				
What have you thought about doing at the end of the semester?				

5. Work with a partner. Compare your charts. Write 6 sentences.

Several students have worked on improving their writing skills.

1. _____

2. _____

3. _____

4. _____

5. _____

6. _____

KEEP GOING!

Do you think it's possible to set too many goals? Why or why not?

Talk about your opinions with the class.

You're Doing a Great Job!

1. Work with 3 classmates. Say all the lines in the script.
2. Choose your character.
3. Finish the conversation. Write more lines for each character.
4. Practice the lines.
5. Act out the role-play with your group.

Scene

A sales meeting

Characters

- Sales Manager
- Salesperson 1
- Salesperson 2
- Salesperson 3

Props

- A clipboard
- Pads of paper
- Pens

The Script

Sales Manager: I want to congratulate all of you on doing a great job!

Salesperson 1: Thank you for saying so.

Salesperson 2: Yes. That's really good to hear.

Sales Manager: You've done a great job of increasing sales. I value that.

Salesperson 3: Thanks.

Sales Manager: I'd like to see improvement, though, in dealing with phone orders. Some customers have complained about waiting a long time for their orders to arrive.

Salesperson 1: Oh, we didn't realize there was a problem.

Salesperson 3: Sometimes the items they ordered are sold out.

Sales Manager: I recommend checking that we have the item while the customer is still on the phone.

Salesperson 2: That's a good idea. Is there anything else we should work on?

KEEP GOING!

Watch your classmates' role-plays. Write the answers to these questions: What else does the sales manager want the salespeople to do? What do the salespeople say?

Pair A: Old Products, New Ideas

1. Find a partner with page 134. You are Pair A.

2. Read the article.

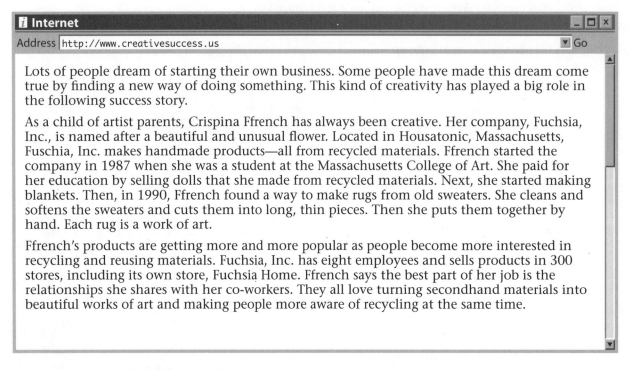

Lots of people dream of starting their own business. Some people have made this dream come true by finding a new way of doing something. This kind of creativity has played a big role in the following success story.

As a child of artist parents, Crispina Ffrench has always been creative. Her company, Fuchsia, Inc., is named after a beautiful and unusual flower. Located in Housatonic, Massachusetts, Fuschia, Inc. makes handmade products—all from recycled materials. Ffrench started the company in 1987 when she was a student at the Massachusetts College of Art. She paid for her education by selling dolls that she made from recycled materials. Next, she started making blankets. Then, in 1990, Ffrench found a way to make rugs from old sweaters. She cleans and softens the sweaters and cuts them into long, thin pieces. Then she puts them together by hand. Each rug is a work of art.

Ffrench's products are getting more and more popular as people become more interested in recycling and reusing materials. Fuchsia, Inc. has eight employees and sells products in 300 stores, including its own store, Fuchsia Home. Ffrench says the best part of her job is the relationships she shares with her co-workers. They all love turning secondhand materials into beautiful works of art and making people more aware of recycling at the same time.

3. Answer the QUESTIONS FOR PAIR A together.

QUESTIONS FOR PAIR A

    a. What does Crispina Ffrench's company sell?

_____

    b. How does Ffrench make her rugs?

_____

    c. Why are Fuchsia, Inc.'s products getting more and more popular?

_____

4. Find a Pair B with page 135. Answer their questions about your article.

5. Ask them the QUESTIONS TO ASK PAIR B. Write their answers.

QUESTIONS TO ASK PAIR B

    a. What does David Riegert's company do?

_____

    b. How do customers get designs on their own jeans?

_____

    c. For Riegert, what is the best part of his job?

_____

KEEP GOING!

Talk about the businesses you read about. Why do you think they are successful? What kind of people do you think their customers are?

Pair B: Old Products, New Ideas

1. Find a partner with page 135. You are Pair B.

2. Read the article.

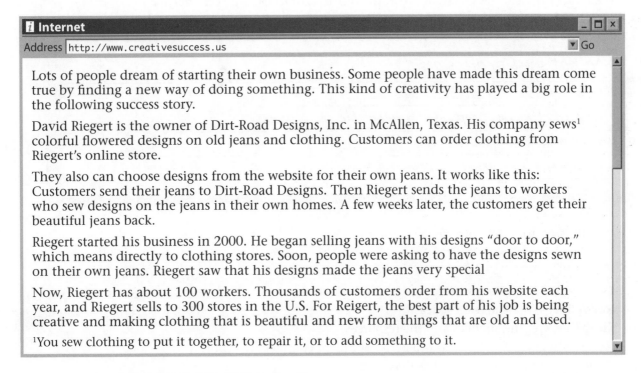

Lots of people dream of starting their own business. Some people have made this dream come true by finding a new way of doing something. This kind of creativity has played a big role in the following success story.

David Riegert is the owner of Dirt-Road Designs, Inc. in McAllen, Texas. His company sews[1] colorful flowered designs on old jeans and clothing. Customers can order clothing from Riegert's online store.

They also can choose designs from the website for their own jeans. It works like this: Customers send their jeans to Dirt-Road Designs. Then Riegert sends the jeans to workers who sew designs on the jeans in their own homes. A few weeks later, the customers get their beautiful jeans back.

Riegert started his business in 2000. He began selling jeans with his designs "door to door," which means directly to clothing stores. Soon, people were asking to have the designs sewn on their own jeans. Riegert saw that his designs made the jeans very special

Now, Riegert has about 100 workers. Thousands of customers order from his website each year, and Riegert sells to 300 stores in the U.S. For Reigert, the best part of his job is being creative and making clothing that is beautiful and new from things that are old and used.

[1]You sew clothing to put it together, to repair it, or to add something to it.

3. Answer the QUESTIONS FOR PAIR B together.

QUESTIONS FOR PAIR B

    a. What does David Riegert's company do?

    _____

    b. How do customers get designs on their own jeans?

    _____

    c. For Riegert, what is the best part of his job?

    _____

4. Find a Pair A with page 134. Ask them the QUESTIONS TO ASK PAIR A. Write their answers.

QUESTIONS TO ASK PAIR A

    a. What does Crispina Ffrench's company sell?

    _____

    b. How does Ffrench make her rugs?

    _____

    c. Why are Fuchsia, Inc.'s products getting more and more popular?

    _____

5. Answer Pair A's questions about your article.

KEEP GOING!

Talk about the businesses you read about. Why do you think they are successful?
What kind of people do you think their customers are?

What's My Profession?

The Project: Create a guessing game about professions
Supplies: index cards or slips of paper, pens or markers
Resources: dictionaries, the Occupations topic of the *Oxford Picture Dictionary*, classified job ads, or other lists of occupations

	What's my profession?
	I'm a high school graduate.
	I'm good at making people feel comfortable and welcome.
	I like meeting new people.
	I have experience answering phones in an office.

1. Work with 3–5 students. Introduce yourself.

2. Choose your job.

> **Leader:** Help your team work together and watch the time.
> **Recorder:** Write the team's ideas.
> **Supplier:** Get the supplies and the resources.
> **Researcher:** Find information to help your team complete the project.
> **Reporter:** Tell the class about the project.

3. As a group, choose 5 professions. Don't tell the other teams about your choices.

4. Brainstorm answers to this question: What personal qualities, education, achievements and experience are needed for these professions?

> **Leader:** Give the team 5 minutes. Ask each person the question.
> **Recorder:** Write the name and answers of each team member.
> **Researcher:** Find more information to help your team complete the project.

5. Create the game.

> **Supplier:** Get the supplies and the resources from your teacher.
> **Team:**
> - Make 1 card for each profession.
> - Write the name of the profession on one side of the card.
> - Write *What's my profession?* at the top of the other side of the card.
> - Write sentences about the qualities, education, achievements, and experience needed for your profession.
>
> **Researcher:** Use a dictionary to help your team with vocabulary and spelling.

6. Show your project to the class.

> **Reporter:** Read your team's cards to the class. Ask your classmates to guess the profession.

KEEP GOING!

Write sentences about the qualities, education, achievements, and experience needed for a profession that you'd like to have.

© Oxford University Press • Permission granted to reproduce for classroom use.